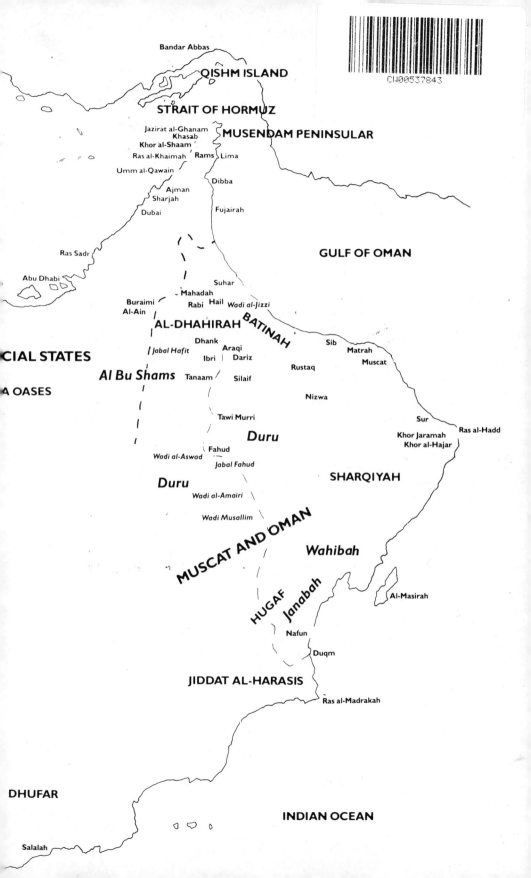

THIS STRANGE EVENTFUL HISTORY

THIS STRANGE EVENTFUL HISTORY

Memoirs of Earlier Days in the UAE and Oman

EDWARD HENDERSON

QUARTET BOOKS
LONDON   NEW YORK

My sincere appreciation must be recorded for the work done so well for me in typing the manuscript by Grethe Jeberg and Cynthia Blake.

First published by Quartet Books Ltd 1988
A member of the Namara Group
27/29 Goodge Street, London W1P 1FD

British Library Cataloguing in Publication Data

Henderson, Edward
This strange eventful history: memoirs of
earlier days in the UAE and Oman.
1. Arab countries, ca. 1940s
I. Title
909'.0974927

ISBN 0-7043-2671-X

Typeset by AKM Associates (UK) Ltd
Ajmal House, Hayes Road, Southall, London
Printed and bound in Great Britain at
The Camelot Press plc, Southampton

Contents

BURAIMI FALAJES

Falaj ...

Cleaning complete ...

Underground crossing ...

The *falajes* where they flow underground were mapped by the author in 1955 when he superintended their cleaning. The area of each palm grove is outlined. The houses (not shown) were at points on the edges of the groves.

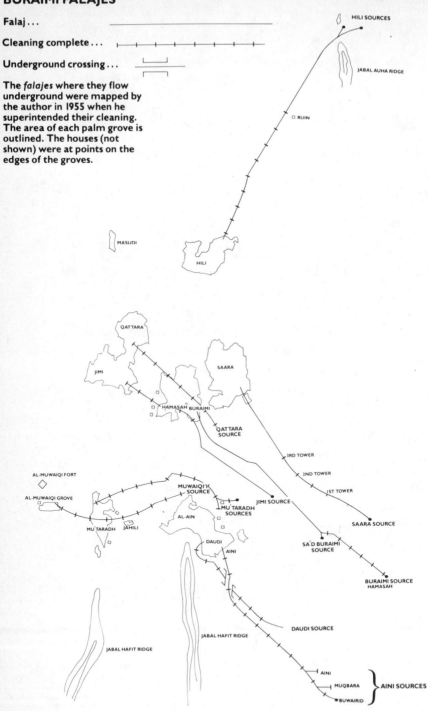

Dedication

I dedicate this book to His Highness Shaikh Zayed bin
Sultan al-Nahyan as an expression of my gratitude for
his friendship and encouragement over so many years.

Note

In spelling names I have tended to keep with modern practice. I have not used accents to differentiate Arab letters which have no English equivalent. Many names are customarily written in English omitting the Arabic definite article. For example al-Sharjah is now commonly written Sharjah in place of Ash Shariqah, also I have al-Hasa for al-Asha, and Buraimi for al-Buraimi.

Preface

By His Excellency Ahmed Khalifa al-Suaidi

Edward Henderson came to the Trucial Coast in 1948 in the service of Petroleum Development Trucial Coast. Later he entered the British Foreign Service (1956–74) and he ended his career in the service as the first British Ambassador to independent Qatar. Since 1976 he has been a member of the Centre for Documentation and Research in Abu Dhabi.

The book covers in detail the years 1948–56 and then brings the story up to date with the discovery of oil and its consequences. These years were the best ones both for the Arabs and Britain and it was not until 1971 that the British decided to leave peacefully. As a result, Edward Henderson, both in the search for oil and as a diplomat, did not feel any of the pull of dual loyalty which often confronted British officers during the nineteenth century. Thus it was natural that Edward Henderson was able to befriend and work with the shaikhs of the Emirates and also with the people; he has a close friendship with His Highness Shaikh Zayed bin Sultan al-Nahyan. His academic achievements in the Centre for Documentation and Research and his lectures in the United States (1982–3) enlightening the American public have been much appreciated by His Highness Shaikh Zayed, as well as by academic scholars. I am sure that scholars and diplomats among others will find these memoirs useful and fascinating.

Foreword

By the late Sir David Roberts

Edward Henderson's fascinating book tells two important political stories; and a lot more besides.

First, there is the story of how the Sultan of Muscat was enabled to establish a united state of Muscat and Oman with oil reserves to propel its primitive economy into take-off and to play a vital role in the security of the Arabian Peninsula. For centuries the authority of the Sultan of Muscat over the interior of his country had been precarious, since it was disputed by the Ibadhi Imams. The whole history of Oman is characterized by a series of Imamates in Ibadhi tradition with a number of intervening years without an Imam when the state was still regarded as viable.

The capital was always in the interior until 1748. When the present dynasty drove out the Persians in the middle of the eighteenth century they put the capital on the coast in Muscat and kept it there. This succeeded under strong Sultans but not under the strongest of all, Saiyid Said (1807–56), because of his preoccupation with empire building in Africa. The interior became more and more independent. In the nineteenth century there were short periods of union and longer periods of partial dis-union. In 1913 the interior based on the highland area revolted and only the British saved the Sultan. In 1921 a curious agreement was made at Sib by which the interior became semi-autonomous. (The Iraq Petroleum Company [IPC] had a concession with the Sultan before the Second World War; but the problem was that the Sultan and his government had very little authority inland and he and his ministers and officials were not allowed to visit it.) Under a sort of *modus vivendi* the Imam's people had Muscat passports, paid customs on entry of goods and could go to the Muscat appeal court. Otherwise they were virtually independent.

In the 1950s an Ibadhi Imam, supported by money and arms from Saudi Arabia, attempted to assert complete independence of the Sultan. Edward Henderson, representing the Iraq Petroleum Company, intrigued with the shaikhs of one of the leading tribes (the Duru) and in effect persuaded them to acknowledge the Sultan's rule and thus create the minimum of stability required before a company would incur the expense and risk of drilling for oil. He succeeded in the teeth of the Sultan's refusal to support his operations, indeed his actual veto against any operations. As a result the Sultan's authority was established (although only after some spectacular operations by the SAS) and oil was found. Throughout this period Henderson acted as an independent agent to promote what he believed to be British and Omani interests. He was proved right.

The second story, also set in the 1950s, is the capture and the pacification of Buraimi, the name loosely applied to a large oasis in the north of Oman which is an equivalent of Crewe Junction to the communications of the desert and lies amid rich oilfields. An armed Saudi band, with the support of an American oil company eager for new concessions, had taken control of Buraimi in breach of a Standstill Agreement between the British Government, acting on behalf of the Sultan of Muscat, and the Ruler of Abu Dhabi. A British expedition of Trucial Oman Levies captured Buraimi and removed the Saudis and their supporters. Henderson accompanied the expedition as Political Officer charged to prevent bloodshed. This succeeded and a further step was taken towards the security of this strategic area. The author is very modest indeed about his own doings, but I know from British and Arab participants that he played a conspicuous part in these important events.

So steeped is he in the tradition of the area that he writes exactly like a Bedu telling a tale in a *majlis* or round a fire in the desert. But he also conveys a vast quantity of information about tribal customs and history which anyone who has had to deal with that part of the world will recognize as of inestimable value. Those of us who served in the Gulf always knew that the Gulf Arabs and their ways of doings things were an intricate speciality within the wider speciality of the Arab world. A diplomat might speak excellent Arabic and have deep experience of the Levant or Egypt or the Maghreb, but he would need at least six months before he could comport himself in a *majlis* or at an Arab feast and even longer before he could arbitrate with confidence between two contending

Rulers in a dispute over land or water. When I was Ambassador to the United Arab Emirates in Abu Dhabi from 1977–81 I always told any visiting British official or businessman that if he wished to apply himself seriously to Abu Dhabi he must first carry in his head the family tree of the al-Nahayyan family; otherwise he would simply not understand the personalities or their motives for action. Edward has captured not only the detail of this world but the authentic flavour of the Arabs of the area. I would urge any young diplomat or businessman who aspired to work effectively in the area to read this book *slowly* and at leisure; and to dip back into it from time to time.

I first knew Edward when I was Political Agent in the Trucial States, based in Dubai from 1966–8; and he used to visit us from Bahrain, where he was on the Political Resident's staff. It was quickly clear to me that I could learn from an hour's talk with him what it would take me weeks and some luck to find out for myself. He could walk in unannounced, just as the Bedu do in their curiously democratic way, into the *majlis* of any Ruler the length of the Gulf, a privilege enjoyed by few Britons indeed. My great friend and mentor, the late Geoffrey Arthur, held the same view of Edward as I did.

I heartily commend this book by a valued friend and colleague of many years' standing. We can all learn from a man who quietly belongs to the long tradition of British explorers of the Arabian Peninsula, and who can truthfully say, 'I have done the State some service; and they know it.'

Introduction

There have been dramatic changes throughout the world over the last twenty to thirty years, but has any one of them been as startling and remarkable in its effects as those which took place in the country which is now the United Arab Emirates and in the neighbouring state Oman? Our first reaction must be 'Thank God it all happened'. That is the heartfelt sentiment which runs through this story. Much has been written of the economic, social and material advances that have been so quickly made in those states, but do we yet have a picture of what it felt like to the people of these countries (and to any one who was involved with them right through this time up to the present)? The changes in the Gulf were entirely different from those which took place elsewhere in the world.

We have seen the astonishingly quick development of 'new towns' in Europe and America, but these places were built in a 'developed' country; services were available, so were materials, machinery, engineers, workers and all the necessary communication network. Anyone can build a new town if he has a big bank balance, but supposing he has no bank, nowhere for imported engineers, managers, skilled tradesmen, doctors, nurses and so on to live, and only a tiny labour force with no skilled workers at all to draw on. In the shaikhdoms as late as the 1950s there were no medical services, no port to land machinery and equipment, no electricity, bridges or roads. Add to this one of the fiercest summer climates in the world and you have what we are inclined to call 'a problem'. Imagine a population explosion in Abu Dhabi shaikhdom from (say) forty thousand in 1960 to over half a million by 1984, and more than double that for the whole country in less than twenty-five years. This vastly increased population now has every modern facility to be found in any top-standard-of-living country in the world; here you have something you can safely call an achievement.

I lived inside this turmoil, always amazed, always slightly unbelieving; yet it is all true and it has happened and the people of the shaikhdoms are naturally very happy that this is so. Both the nationals and the expatriates had to work very hard to find and produce the oil which made it all possible, and then work even harder to achieve all this development so quickly and so well. Part of the story I found most exciting, all of it fascinating, as I lived through it and saw and heard it all happening. I hope also to give some idea of how the people of the area emerged after suffering the hardship of a terrible economic depression and how they all worked to turn the riches from underground, which annoyingly we never actually see, into a new reality above ground and into happiness for their children. Credit for all this must go to the people who carried out the work, to the experts from abroad who brought in the necessary technical expertise, and above all to the leaders whose inspiration made it all possible. Most of these I am happy to say, are still with us.

The first three chapters describe the Trucial Coast area as I saw it in 1948 when I first came to the Gulf as the representative of the oil company which had the concession to explore the Trucial Coast and Oman. Chapter four tells how I came to join the oil company and what our aims were. The later chapters tell of our difficulties over the entry into the hinterland of Oman, and the surprising things that happened to us in our search for oil. Our journeys in central Oman were the first ever made by a foreign expedition with motor vehicles. Previous visits by Westerners on camels can be counted on the fingers of one hand. Our expedition to Fahud was to alter the whole history of Oman. How this happened has never been described before. These events were not without excitement and I hope something of this will be reflected in these pages.

1

The Trucial States Before Oil

When I first came to it in 1948, the coast looked very different from the way it does today. Seen from the air, on a clear day, it was a wide landscape of sand and mud-flat dotted in some parts with bushes and trees, which appeared simply as black dots in the sand, while the most prominent features inland were the ridges of sand, in some places stretching for miles in graceful curves, at others broken and disturbed. The coast was edged with its white lines of surf, looking motionless from above, that divided the blue of the sea from the brownish yellow of the foreshore. Away to the north and east the jagged peaks of the main Oman range of mountains broke the curve of the horizon. The coast-line was breached in several places by creeks which seemed to have punched their way through the shore-line to find their way inland, to be finally soaked up in the sandy waste. Dark patches, which were mangroves, could be seen among some of the winding creeks. Those creeks which were deep enough to take in country craft, the sailing boats of the Gulf, had become the *raison d'être* for small ports whose low white buildings and palm-branch huts clustered round the water's edge. These ports, which were the only centres of population on the coast itself, looked very small from the air, as if man could only maintain a feeble hold on the edge of the desert.

Towards the west the population was mainly from the Bani Yas, an Arab tribe, some settled, some seamen, some bedouin. To the north-east of them were mixed tribes ruled largely by the Qawasim or Jowasim. In Abu Dhabi other tribes had also adhered to the main Bani Yas group in that they acknowledged the shaikh as their paramount and yet had not merged themselves with the tribe but kept their separate identity. In the last part of the eighteenth century and the early years of the nineteenth, the Bani Yas in Abu Dhabi and Dubai were under the one Shaikh of Abu

Dhabi. The Dubai Bani Yas broke away from Abu Dhabi more than once and after 1833 became separate under their own shaikh who came from the Al bu Falasah section of the Bani Yas.

The Bani Yas of Abu Dhabi were occupied both in the desert and at sea, and were settled in Abu Dhabi itself and in al-Ain. Their main occupations at sea were pearl diving and fishing, and they also sailed their country craft across the Gulf. Some of them settled in summer in the Liwa oases, where they grew dates and reared camels, sheep and goats. Those in Dubai were similarly occupied, but the port was growing in size and steamships called regularly at Dubai, lying off-shore to unload into barges.

Further to the east were the Qawasim in Sharjah and beyond them the smaller shaikhdoms of Ajman and Umm al-Qawain, and eastward again was Ras al-Khaimah ruled by another branch of the Qawasim. (In the past Sharjah and Ras al-Khaimah had been one shaikhdom.) Round the corner on the Gulf of Oman was Fujairah at that time not yet recognized as a separate shaikhdom by the British and with whom my company did not yet have a concession.

In the eighteenth century Britain had kept the peace at sea with warships based on India, and in the Gulf itself on Bushire on the Iranian coast. In 1820, after hostilities with the Qawasim and the British capture of Ras al-Khaimah, treaties were signed with all six lower-Gulf shaikhdoms which created a special treaty relationship with these shaikhdoms by the terms of which Britain provided defence and left the shaikhs very considerable independence in their own administration.

The tribes of these eastern shaikhdoms were partly concerned with the sea (especially the Qawasim), occupied with pearl-diving, fishing and coastal trading, and partly with the land as bedouins and semi-settled or settled farmers. Steamships also called at Sharjah but not at any other port between Sharjah and Muscat.

Until 1947, when India became independent, the Arab states of the Gulf, with the exception of what is now Saudi Arabia and Iraq, were connected to the British Indian administration. They were managed in a somewhat similar way to the separate princely states in India which were ruled by their Rajahs with British officials at their side to advise. In the Gulf, however, the position was slightly different because the British government of India seemed anxious to have as little as possible to do with the internal affairs of the Gulf states and as far as was practical would deal only with foreign affairs and defence. Consequently British officials were resident in a few places only in the nineteenth century and also through the opening years of this century. The various treaties of the nineteenth and twentieth centuries between HMG and the shaikhs gave Britain great power, but she accepted very limited responsibility. This remained the case right up to the withdrawal of the British in 1971, largely through what had become a customary acceptance of a position that allowed the shaikhly governments very great freedom in their internal affairs while the British provided secure defence to the whole region as well as peace at sea. Only at a very few points in the period 1820–1948 was it felt necessary to provide a land force anywhere in the Gulf and peace was kept by the Bombay Marine (later the Indian Navy) backed as necessary by the Royal Navy.

In the nineteenth century there was supposed to be a squadron of six small ships allocated to the Gulf but this was often only on paper, and we can read of a Political Resident in Bushire in the middle of the nineteenth century complaining that no ship had visited him for two years. For much of that century the British government of India had only three posts manned permanently in the Gulf by British officials: Muscat, Bushire and Basrah (and not always Muscat). There was a locally engaged Residency Agent, with very limited powers, in Sharjah from 1823. After the campaign of 1820 which established the British treaty connection with what became known later as the Trucial Coast, British or Indian troops visited the Gulf very seldom, and then only to deal with external threats, such as happened in the two world wars. In the 1930s RAF landing strips were made, and in the Second World War RAF and US Air Force aircraft were stationed in the Gulf. (In Oman itself there were two occasions in the nineteenth century and several in the twentieth when the British intervened ashore, at the Sultan's request.)

By 1948 when I arrived the British had reduced their presence to the Royal Air Force landing grounds at Bahrain and Sharjah, the latter manned by a small ground staff and one officer. No aircraft were then kept stationed in the Gulf. When I first came the army was represented in Bahrain by one charming and amusing and very Irish Brigadier, Robert Baird, who greeted me with the news one day that the strength of the British army had been doubled overnight. 'The Lord save us, me boy, me batman's arrived.'

The coming of the oil industry, first to Bahrain in 1932, had started a gradual change. The various treaties had earlier established the practice of the British of administering judicial courts in regard only to cases concerning certain categories of foreigners. It was originally intended to cover the British themselves and those of Indian nationality. In many shaikhdoms there were so few involved that courts were not set up and visiting British officials (or where there were any, resident ones) dealt with cases. With the coming of many foreign companies the situation changed and for this reason the British found themselves with the choice of either bringing in more administrators and judges or giving up these practices to which they laid claim by treaty. They chose to strengthen their position by increasing staff and setting up permanent courts which could be visited by a judge periodically. In addition to the legal issue, many other administrative matters came up which involved more British officials and it is ironic that it was only towards the as yet unforseen end of the British hegemony in the Gulf that their presence became much more obvious, especially in Bahrain where they had their military and political headquarters.

The two world wars of this century largely passed the Trucial States by. For a short time a tiny airstrip was made and used in the Dubai area. Sharjah strip was important as a landing ground for aircraft ferrying to India and the Far East, but by 1948 the Trucial States had forgotten the world war which had meant no more to them than the wartime rice and sugar quota, designed to prevent shortages of basic foods. The war had, however, deepened the economic recession which had started in about 1929.

The arrival of the British-India steamer was an occasion in Dubai and Sharjah. The 'goer-up' or the 'goer-down', as the ship was called, would anchor about a mile or more out to sea, and small boats would scurry out to bring her passengers ashore. The majority of these country craft were *jalboots* (from the English 'jolly-boat'), short, stumpy, wooden sailing ships with a vertical plank for a prow, a single mast and a lateen sail. More and more of these little boats were being fitted with small diesel engines. There was one which we used to charter from time to time for carrying Company stores up and down the coast and for our own journeys. She was called *Shaheen*, the Arabic word for falcon, and had a crew of five. When on board, we lived on deck, and I used to sleep on an air mattress since I found the lurching of a camp-bed intolerable; in anything of a sea it was a case of lying on the bare deck anyway.

In addition to these small boats, there were the much bigger *booms* which would sail from Kuwait to Dubai and southwards as far as Zanzibar. These were often two-masted and the habit of fitting an engine was at that time just beginning; even those so fitted would use their sails as well if the wind was favourable. They were long, beautiful ships with their billowing lateen sails and purposeful raked prows. Dubai creek was an endless joy to watch. Apart from little *jalboots* fussing up and down with the pug pug of their little engines, there were the larger country craft plying the creek at high tide, majestically under sail. On each occasion they would have to pull in the sail and furl it on the spar, pushing it under and past the mast which, with lateen rig, is raked steeply forwards, and set it in order to go right about on the other tack to catch the wind and fill the sail as the helm went hard over for the bend. Among them scurried little *abaras*, two-oared ferry boats, literally 'crossers'. There were hundreds of them in those days, and none of them had motors. They would ply as taxis across the creek or up and down it, since all the houses were in those days close to the creek side.

The town was divided into three districts. The oil company house where I lived in Dubai was on the south side, to the north of us was Deira, then a growing community but no bigger than Dubai, and to the north-west was Shandagha, a purely residential district on the same bank as Dubai, but sometimes cut off like an island when a high tide and strong wind coincided. There some of the shaikhs lived, but in very modest 'palaces' indeed. One of these old houses was used by Shaikh Said, the Ruler, as his chief residence.

On the Deira side there was an increasing number of cars, perhaps two dozen by 1948; and on the Dubai side, the shaikh had two or three. The oil company had five cars, mainly for inland expeditions. The track outside our house disappeared almost at once into the cavern of the souk, the market, which was not then wide enough for cars to enter. The traffic in front of our house was limited to donkeys and foot passengers, but noisy and busy it was. The town noises were punctuated all day by an old beggar, sitting a little way down our street, whose strange cry was rather distressing until you became used to it. He seemed to collect quite a lot of money, much of it in the tiniest coins of all, worth about a farthing, and we contributed regularly as he, as it were, belonged to us.

At our door sat Ghanim bin Ali, a genial man but nearly blind, much mocked at by his friends because he had nine daughters and no sons. He was our chief guard; we had two others, not that they had any guarding to do, but they seemed to be necessary appurtenances to a house in those days. They helped to keep away small boys if they became too bothersome and noisy. More important, they kept us in touch with local events and advised us on social etiquette.

Dubai souk was about two hundred yards long, covered-over and dark, with the shops on either side of a central lane. Each shop was a small rectangle, the back being in darkness. At its entrance sat the owner, cross-legged on the ground, with the more attractive and recently bought wares around him. If you wished to buy, he would offer you a small stool or the corner of the rug on which he sat, and then he plied you with coffee, or if he was an Iranian merchant, with sweet tea. The souk had a subdued hubbub about it, for this was before the days of transistor radios. The strolling crowds, almost all in long Arab *thawbs*, or robes, made a murmur of voices punctuated every now and then by a small boy on a bicycle much too large for him, warning of his headlong approach with a squeaky horn.

The shops were varied: in one, meat would be cooking, while next to it another would stock a pile of dented tins of soup, baked beans or sardines. The next shop might be an Indian tailor or a cloth shop, but many sold a little of everything so that at first sight these dungeon-like cavities seemed unlikely to have what you wanted but often, after the shopkeeper had rummaged about in the dark recesses, he would pull out the article you were looking for. The drawback to this was that the farther back in the shop the article was found, the older it would be, as fresh goods always took pride of place at the front.

If you could not find what you wanted on the Dubai side, you would walk through the half light to the end of the souk, where suddenly you were faced by a dazzling and raucous opening between the houses, and you were at the water's edge. Here bumping against the rough stone steps, would be twenty or thirty little *abara* boats, jostling for custom. As soon as anyone appeared from the darkness of the souk, anyone who looked a likely customer, the *abara* men would all shout together, each one certain that his eloquent persuasion would induce you to pick his boat.

Once aboard, the excitement died; the *abara* man would push the boat out and his competitors would give him a friendly shove from either side. Then, in a standing, stooping position he would push, not pull, at the oars which were each tied by a loop of rope to a wooden pin stuck through the gunwale. In this way, the boat would go quite fast over the choppy little waves of the turquoise blue creek, whose sudden brightness was cheerful after the gloom of the souk. The journey took you a little further up the creek, as the other *abara* station in Deira was not opposite the one in Dubai.

A little beyond on the right could be seen the long building of the Ruler's old palace. Of two storeys, with a plaster-decorated front, and with verandahs the whole length on each floor, it looked imposing simply because it was the biggest building, and it had an almost quaintly Victorian look about it; but it also looked unused and decayed. Next to it was the Customs office where the Ruler's son, Shaikh Rashid, held court on the verandah. In front of the office was a wharf and on it a small iron crane with a hand crank, and there were always some small barges moored alongside. It was not until I had been in Dubai for some time that I discovered that the lower floor of the old palace itself was absolutely full of merchandise. In particular the first sacks of cement were here, the cement which was shortly to transform Dubai.

Meanwhile, the *abara* man had rowed the little boat almost to the other side of the creek, at the same time keeping up a running conversation to describe to his fare the events of the day and his philosophy of life. The first thing to be seen as one bumped through the crowd of boats at the Deira *abara* station was the British Bank of the Middle East's very special lavatory. I always thought the boat would hit it, but it never did. The bank itself was right on the creek's edge to the left of the landing point. It was a modest single-storey building with windows on to the creek and its chief ornament was its lavatory which was really no more than a platform sticking out over the water, with the essential slit in its middle, tastefully boxed in and screened from view with palm branches. Whoever was inside had a rather broken view of the outside world, but the outside world could not see in.

If Deira-bound it would be an automatic drill to drop in and pass the time of day with Mark Stott, the bank manager, and at that time our only European colleague in Dubai. His bank was in Deira, but he then lived at the RAF mess in Sharjah. Not only was his lavatory odd, but his office had an unusual feature. At his back, set in the window, was a fan run by a tiny paraffin engine which went clank, clank, clank, and turned a small blade round, it seemed to me, very slowly. I always maintained that the paraffin engine made more trouble with its heat and smell, than any comfort it could provide, as it brought in the remarkably unfresh air from the creek in tiny quantities. However, Mark robustly held that it made life bearable and he would not be without it for anything. He was a hefty, solid and jolly man, much more like a cavalry officer than a banker; it was a pleasure to exchange gossip with him and sip a glass of rather warm lime juice, for like all of us he had no refrigerator.

From Mark's hospitable office we would go through the souk to a tiny square and thence into a choice of dark entrances. One was for cloth, one was for household goods, another for carpentry and so on. These souks were long, narrow tunnels of dark alleyways, arranged on the standard Eastern style, each reserved to its trade, miniatures of the arcaded souks of Aleppo or Cairo. The cloth souk was cool and comparatively quiet and was heavy with the smell of camphor in the new bales of cloth. Others were redolent of spice, of cooked meat, or of tobacco. The alleys were narrow and small but they had great character, and the shopkeepers, naturally glad to see a customer, made you very welcome. Whether you bought or not, it was impossible to stop without taking coffee or tea. Those who wished to gossip could do so there all day.

A very important feature of the souk in 1948 was the nature of the things on display. Even in Dubai, which had closer contact with the outside world than the other places, very little of the goods available came from factories abroad. Almost all the foodstuff was simply in its natural state with no packaging. As the years went by more packaged goods, and advertisements came to these souks. This altered their character completely. This was especially so in the interior of Oman, for example, where in a busy market, up to the 1960s, nothing would be on sale which betrayed its foreign origin, and most things would be locally made or grown. Now not only the appearance but the whole atmosphere of the market has changed. I no longer feel I am really abroad and in a strange place because I see all around me the things I would buy in the West.

In 1948, so far had modernity reached Dubai, the occasional car would force its way down the road from the bank since it was just, but only just, wide enough. On either side there were low stone or mud-brick buildings, mostly shops, work-shops and storehouses. The road was roofed over, and a car would come honking down it disturbing the walker, and those sitting outside the shops would have to grab their stools and retreat indoors until the car had passed. The crowds which wandered in this street, like the others, would mainly be Arabs in white *thawbs* or robes, and those who were the Ruler's men would carry their rifles and wear curved daggers at their belts. There were also Indians, Pakistanis and Iranians, but the Arabs were the distinctive figures, and in those days everyone wore their traditional national dress. The Arabs from Oman wore coloured *thawbs*, and bright Kashmiri scarves wound round their heads like an untidy but colourful turban. The men walked gracefully with short steps, heads held back and slim bodies graceful and lithe, as did the women from the habit of carrying loads on their heads.

Then there were the bedouin from nearby tribes like the Manasir. They showed their pride, and the young bloods would strut through the town as if they owned it. At that time, they were not allowed to walk in town armed, but they were always armed when they went out into the desert. Even without their rifles they had a roguish, attractively over-confident air because the bedouin all looked down on the townsmen. The shaikhs of all the towns on the coast, mainly bedouin by descent, still very much affected bedouin ways, and they could, therefore, keep on easy terms with the desert folk, although they were half-way to being townsmen. Respect for the bedouin was more particularly marked in Abu Dhabi, but along the whole coast the bedouin were the aristocrats and the ancestors of many of the shaikhly families were from the wholly nomadic tribes of the interior.

I called one day on a merchant friend who has since become remarkably rich. After the usual coffee and tea, I started to ask idly about his business and what he traded in. 'I trade in everything that comes to hand,' he smiled. 'Come and look at this.' He took me out of the shop, round a corner and up a back alleyway. He came to a door and shouted. Up sprung a boy, it seemed from nowhere. 'Please open it up,' he ordered. A small postern was opened which was set within two big double doors, and I was shown inside. When I got used to the dim light, I could see we were in a long low mud-brick warehouse completely full of bicycles. 'But,' I said in amazement, 'there are no roads here and very few people ride bicycles.' 'My friend,' replied the merchant smiling, 'of course I shall not sell them here, one or two perhaps. I shall ship them into Pakistan. This is how I got a similar number of Singer sewing machines off my hands in this same way.'

Some of the stone or coral and plaster houses on both sides of the creek had the picturesque and stately wind-towers called *badgirs*, of Persian origin, which were found then on both sides of the Gulf. They look rather like our own village church towers and are attractively decorated with ornamentation in plaster. These are efficient as a means of cooling the rooms below, as the four sides are really scoops designed to push the wind downward into the house, the force being controlled by wooden shutters on each of the four sides which can be closed in the cooler weather. From whichever way the wind blows these towers are designed to catch it and bring it into the house: you simply open the appropriate side, leaving the others closed. On a humid day the powerful draught they can produce in the rooms below is very refreshing. On dry days they are not effective, as they need humid air, but it is seldom dry. When there is no wind at all, they are of course useless, and even with all the shutters closed they are very draughty in the winter, as the wind will force its way through.

Our Company house, unfortunately, had no such tower, but the wide verandah which ran its length faced the prevailing north-west wind and there were three passages right through the house to enable the wind to blow across the verandah at these points. Although we were without air-conditioning, or even fans for much of the time I lived there, we usually had a draught of air blowing through the house. The worst times were those frequent nights in the summer when humidity was maximum and the air was too still even to stir the thick mist which rose out of the creek. Maximum shade temperature was 123°F, but normally the day temperature was around 105°F in the summer. The trouble came from the high humidity and from the high night temperatures which in late summer were sometimes not so far below those of the day. After sunset the wind would drop and the humidity would rise even further.

One day in the autumn of 1949 we had the inspiring sight of the pearl boats returning from the *ghaws*, the diving season. Ten major and many smaller boats came into Dubai that year, although this was many fewer than would have been seen in the 1930s and before. We could see the ships lying off the bar waiting to come in on the high tide of the early afternoon, and in the afternoon we put out in an *abara* to watch them come in. The first two were the largest. They set their sails and headed for the bar. As they crossed it, the wind dropped and we could see that instead of relying on sail, they had their long sweeps out, ten to each side in the largest boats, and with three men pushing on each sweep, they crossed the bar and entered the creek at quite a speed. All Dubai was on the banks, or like us, out in small boats to greet them, for they had been away at sea for months. The two leading boats were almost abreast as they rounded the bend and they raced with tremendous vigour, great sheets of water splashing up at every stroke, to the anchorage further in. High in the stern of each was stationed a young lad with a screaming falsetto to urge on the rowers, and the rowers themselves shouted in unison, a harsh menacing cry in rhythm with the thump of the oars. As the boats swept in, one after another, it seemed more like the start of a battle than the end of a long voyage.

Specialist pearl merchants had come from India and Pakistan to examine the catch and make purchases. Shortly after the arrival of the boats, I watched these merchants at work examining and bargaining. One particular merchant would hold court on a verandah overlooking the creek, the merchants and boat owners bringing their pearls to him in large red or yellow cloths which they would spread out on the carpet before him. The old merchant, dressed in the flowing clothes of India, with a white turban-like cloth on his head, would let the pearls trickle through his fingers in a full stream. He looked, and seemed, centuries away from us.

This was the last year that a major fleet went pearling from Dubai, and their numbers have dwindled ever since to almost nothing, partly because of competition from the cultured pearl industry of Japan, partly because this arduous work is unpopular, and now because there are other sources of income available. It is hard to imagine how they lived, each crew, as much as one hundred men, cooped up in a tiny boat, the divers diving all day, never getting ashore for perhaps four months at a time and relying on other boats which brought them food and water. When you are diving you must have an empty stomach so the divers could not eat at all and took only sips of coffee in working hours, that is in daylight, this through the height of the Gulf summer. I was often told stories of the pearling trade. The merchants, of course, operated on the basis of trust in one another, and the habit of honesty in the trade was total. Nothing would ever be put in writing, but everything would be remembered and there were no mistakes in the remembering. Often a particular pearl or a set of pearls would be handed from one merchant to another to sell on his behalf. The pearl might not be sold for a year. When it was sold, the money would simply be handed to the original owner. There might or might not be a commission; it all depended on the relationship of the two merchants.

Pearl diving is a tough profession. I would naturally, but naïvely, ask about the danger from sharks. It was the jellyfish, against which they would sometimes wear a light cotton shirt, that caused them· more trouble, they said. But despite this, I have a friend in Abu Dhabi who in the 1950s was fishing from a boat about a hundred miles down the coast. He was then a lad of sixteen or so and had left the main party anchored just off shore and gone fishing in a small canoe with a companion. They stopped paddling to throw their net, and he had his leg half out of the boat with his foot in the water. Suddenly, a shark leapt out of the water and crunched the canoe and his leg in its jaws. My friend had in his right hand a small iron bar which they used as a sort of anchor for the canoe. He instinctively hit the shark on the nose with it; the shark immediately let go and disappeared. The canoe started to sink, but they were close to the beach. His companion paddled like mad and got to the shore, and bound the hideous wound up with part of their clothing and the anchor cord. The companion then went ashore and walked until he came to the point off shore where the main party had anchored. The ship immediately set sail to rescue the injured man.

Back on the mother ship, the ghastly wounds which stretched from above the knee to the ankle were packed with salty mud. It took a week to get back to Abu Dhabi because of contrary winds. Even back at home there was no better medical aid available, and the poor young man simply lay in his bed, suffering. His amazingly tough constitution, and above all courage, pulled him through. He now walks normally, although his leg is a little wasted, and if you question him, he will cheerfully pull up his *thawb* and show you the livid scars of the shark's teeth, a sharp serrated line down his leg. He cannot be more than fifty years old even now; just to live in those tough old days called for courage.

Wilfred Thesiger was a welcome guest, either at the beginning or at the end of some of his magnificent journeys across the Empty Quarter. He mentions in his book *Arabian Sands* how on one of these occasions he was still accompanied by two of his bedouin who stayed with us in our house, and we introduced them to European food and our ways. I have been many times a guest of the bedouin and as many times entertained them to meals at my house or at a camp in the desert, but this was the only occasion I had real bedouin living with us as house guests in something like a European ménage. As Wilfred recalls, they delighted to waken me before first light with cries of 'Up to pray! Prayer is better than sleep.'

On one of these visits Wilfred and I went down by launch, a *jalboot*, to Abu Dhabi. It was a convenient way to go in those days when Abu Dhabi was still an island, but it meant that when you arrived you had no car, and there were virtually no cars in Abu Dhabi at that time. It was a pleasant, calm trip and took about fourteen hours in the *Shaheen*. On arrival at Abu Dhabi, we anchored off the foreshore and went ashore in the tiny canoe-like dugout through the surf. We walked through the soft sand half a mile or so to the big fort or palace which then seemed to dominate the tiny town (now the town in turn totally dominates it). Shaikh Shakhbut, the Ruler, was at his most charming and courteous and was amused by Wilfred's explanation of my name as meaning 'bin Hender' ('son of Hender' in Arabic), and it is as 'Bin Hender' that I am known to some of the family to this day. Shaikh Shakhbut would hold forth on any subject and had the shrewdest questions to ask, whether about flying saucers or the population of Bristol, the rainfall in Scotland or the politics of the Middle East. We were put in the only substantial house on the seashore, two storeys of mud brick known as Bait al-Shamali, 'the northern house' or the guest house, but most of our meals were taken at the palace, to which we were invited by a messenger on foot. One lunch was at the guest house itself and the Ruler and two of his three brothers came to join us for it, the fourth brother, Shaikh Zayed, being still at al-Ain.

At this point Wilfred and I parted; he to go inland by camel to al-Ain and from there to start one of his journeys, and I to return to Dubai. This was just the first of many interesting and enjoyable visits for me to Abu Dhabi.

Abu Dhabi was in marked contrast to Dubai in those days. Since the death of the great Zayed bin Khalifah in the early years of this century, trading from Abu Dhabi had gone down hill. Moreover, the fall in the pearl trade had hit Abu Dhabi particularly badly. Last century and in the opening decades of this, Abu Dhabi was one of the leading centres for the pearl trade, but by the time I first arrived few ships of any size set forth for the pearl season, and the pearling fleet consisted mainly of small boats which could not venture so far, nor for so long, as in the old days. There was a row of three or four stone-and-plaster-built houses along the front which were then already in ruins. The souk was tiny, and the majority of houses in which the inhabitants lived were of the palm-branch, *barasti* type. The foreshore of the island was three to four miles in length, and the town occupied only a tiny fraction of this. There was a thin scattered line of date palms just inland of the coast, and there was the cluster of huts which formed the town; then near the palm trees, the large fort. The island was in the shape of a narrowing tongue of bare sand and salt-flat surrounded on both sides by wide lagoons and was totally devoid of any vegetation except the thin clumps of desert grasses on a few of the dunes and the dark mangroves in some of the neighbouring lagoons. At its apex, this tongue came near to the mainland, leaving a quarter of a mile or more of shallow sea water which could be forded with difficulty by cars and camels at one place at extreme low tide. Once on the mainland, one's troubles were not over because there were ten miles of salt-flat or *sabkha*, as it is called, which a high tide, a strong wind or rainfall, or worse still, any combination of these, would cover to the depth of a foot or more thus making the going impossible to car and camel alike. Evidence of this lay in the camels' bones which bestrewed it, camels which had fallen in the mud and had broken a limb and had had to be slaughtered ritually and cut up for meat on the spot – the only salvage operation that was possible to recoup a little of their value.

After I had said goodbye to Shaikh Shakhbut and to Wilfred, I sailed back to Dubai in the launch with regret because, despite the simplicity of the place, its very remoteness and the charm of its people were very attractive to me.

2

The Shaikhs and the People
on the Coast and in the Desert

I would visit Abu Dhabi frequently, and soon had a tiny house of mud-brick built there for me. My calls on Shaikh Shakhbut were always interesting and enjoyable.

In the winter and early summer the various shaikhs up and down the coast were sometimes on hunting trips inland and I would be invited to join them for a few days. On one such hunting trip (after I had been several years in the area when more transport was available) I arrived at the small camp in the evening, and was allocated one of the tiny tents. We all dined in the open; the meat served was bustard, recently caught. After dinner the group sat and talked and by about ten o'clock that night I took my leave of the shaikh and retired to my tent. Before dawn there was the call to prayer, and I heard the shaikh and his followers saying the morning prayer in the half light. Then came the merry clink of the brass pestle for grinding coffee and I could smell the coffee fire and thought it right to join them. The shaikh had a happy look in his eye at the prospect of a day's hunting and greeted me warmly. A weak-looking sun had just risen in a cloudy east; it was still winter. We were among beautiful crescent dunes which fell away to the north to the lower rolling sands which lay between us and the sea. This was not the high-dune country of the Empty Quarter, but nevertheless these dunes, some 100–150 feet high, of creamy sand, had the same magic attraction. Their subtle curves, which are accentuated by the shadow cast either by a rising or a setting sun, have a great beauty. Between them in the hollows were the tufts of bush and grasses which one day's rain will create but which may then survive on night dew alone right through a summer.

The shaikh had with him some twenty-five followers and four of the pick-up type trucks. Ten of the followers carried on their arm the *mangal* (glove or leather sleeve), and the lure (a bunch of feathers on a chain) for a falcon. These birds, sitting each on a crooked forearm, seemed alert and ready for a day's sport. Each had a leather hood over its head which its falconer would occasionally remove as if to whet the bird's appetite.

Falconers and followers sat in a ring on the sand, the shaikh in their midst, while the little cups of coffee were handed round. Each cup has only a small amount of coffee, bitter with the cardamom that is in it. As I had found in Syria, it is polite and customary to have the cup refilled twice, and then to shake it between forefinger and thumb to indicate enough. At first, nothing was said. The coffee cups were sucked at meditatively, then the shaikh called his chief tracker and hunter. 'Which way today, oh Salim?'

'May God lengthen your life, the west offers sport. There was good rain there two months ago, about so much.' Here he indicated on his arm a distance of nine inches, showing that the rain had penetrated the sand to that depth. This is the bedouin way of measuring the quantity which had fallen in any one storm. 'The green foliage will be good there, and, God willing, we may see some game.'

'God willing,' said the shaikh and stood up. He motioned me to get into one of the pick-ups with him and the driver (he himself did not drive), and into the back piled several falconers and his chief tracker. Some of the others climbed into a second vehicle and off we set over the dunes, threading our way between their crests towards the west.

The tracker would, from time to time, bang on the roof of the truck and shout fresh instructions. Suddenly he called 'Halt!' He jumped down to examine the tracks of a bustard. Not satisfied that they were less than an hour old, and, therefore, worth following, he jumped back on to the pick-up and off we went again. Some minutes later he banged once more. This time he did not even need to get down, and we too could see fresh tracks. 'Half an hour only,' he cried. 'Follow those.'

Then the car was made to follow the bird's tracks. These led mainly to the hollows of the dunes but sometimes over the crests. To keep the tracks in sight, the driver, Ali, would take abnormal risks and follow a line which made even an agile and tough Chevrolet protest. Occasionally the shaikh would shout, half laughing, 'Oh Ali, have a care!' Salim, from behind, would, on the contrary, shout in protest if the driver went too far from the tracks in order to pick an easier path for his car. It was exhilarating and exciting, but I had nothing to hang on to and was alternately bounced on to the driver and the shaikh. The whole was taken in the highest possible spirits, laughing and shouting; at such moments, the shaikh was no more than one of the boys, the driver taking note only of what Salim said, often ignoring the shaikh's instructions. This went on for some twenty minutes. I was getting bruised, but I had lost my original fear that we should all be overturned.

Suddenly, another bang on the roof and we stopped. All the men were quiet; we jumped down and, at a sign from the shaikh, one of the birds had its hood removed. The falconer stood up in the back of the truck and held it as high as he could. There in the distance I could see two bustard in a hollow grubbing amongst the grasses. These were the birds whose tracks we had been following. The falcon was released, stooped and with a lovely curving, infinitely graceful flight, went right to its prey and, in a great fluttering of wings, seized one of the bustards and dug its beak into the breast again and again. Meanwhile another hawk was released to attack the second bustard which had half flown, half scampered to some larger bushes nearby as if in hope of finding cover. The shaikh and his followers, now all on foot, ran to the scene, and the falconers started to entice their hawks back to the lures with pieces of goat's meat which they had ready as the reward. Trained hawks will hold and wound a bustard without killing provided they can be enticed off the prey in time. It was the custom to cut the bustard's throat and draw blood while it was still alive. I was told that meat from a bird or animal which had been killed by a trained hunting bird of prey (or an animal) is lawful for a Muslim to eat. Hunters, however, always slaughter the prey themselves ritually and train their birds not to kill before they can get there.

The bustard was duly dispatched with a knife and put in the back of the truck. The remaining eight or so falcons on their falconers' arms looked excited under their hoods, their heads going this way and that as if to say, 'Is it my turn next?' After a short break, we climbed aboard again, and the whole process was repeated.

The third kill of the morning was the most exciting. A single bustard was attacked close to some tall tamarisk bushes, and, as the hawk stooped and flew in to the kill, the bustard backed up against a bush and opened its beak in defence. This upset the hawk and, just as a dog which has unexpectedly got to grips with a cat which holds its ground will suddenly pretend to lose all interest and wander off, so it changed course and flew right away. Immediately a second hawk was unhooded and stooped on its prey which was not courageous enough to withstand a second assault. The shaikh told me he had seen two bustard together beat off several hawks but eventually they had succumbed.

I had in earlier years been hawking on camels. That had been even more exciting, much more sporting and difficult. It is undoubtedly a good and exciting sport. It needs skill, especially in the training of the hawks which must be carefully schooled. They are mostly purchased now from the Northern Arab States and Iran, and may fetch enormous prices, but hawks are occasionally still caught in Eastern Arabia. The hawking season in Eastern Arabia is from November to March when the prey, McQueen's bustard, migrate into the area from Russia.

We spent the afternoon inspecting newly dug water wells in the neighbourhood and visiting camps of the bedouin. Only a part of a shaikh's hunting expedition is for amusement. The more important aspect is the chance it gives to visit his people. Different bedouin visit the *majlis* at his camp fire each evening and tell him their woes and ask for help in various ways. In the desert, the subject sits next to the shaikh or in front of him and addresses him by his first name only, seldom using his title. His talk will be a mixture of information and aphorisms and, with many a 'May Allah lengthen your life', will usually end with some form of request for help. The popularity and strength of a shaikh must depend on his accessibility and the wisdom of his manner of treating his subjects. If, as until so recently, he has little money himself, he needs very considerable intelligence, leadership and good sense to hold his people together and make the best use of his meagre resources. If he suddenly hits oil, as has happened recently in the Arabian Gulf, his problems are as suddenly altered but not made more easy. They will become even more acute; but in the early stages at least of the development of the new society, the *majlis* will be the main institution on which the shaikh must rely.

It is fascinating to watch a capable Ruler dealing with his people in his way, off the cuff and in public. He has to have a ready answer to each question or request, and at times he has to make what are really life and death decisions. The shaikh of a nomad tribe has to decide on the spot what is to be done in cases of murder, or war, or feuding. The settled shaikh has his *qadhis* (judges) to help him, but the true nomad does not have professional help, unless he has tied himself in some form of alliance or allegiance to the nearest settled chieftain or uses him as a referee as is sometimes the custom. He will also use *urf* (customary law) which is akin to Islamic law.

As usual, the party all gathered for coffee after evening prayers which were said by the shaikh and his followers standing in a line on the sand. At prayer time, as in so many other ways, Muslims are egalitarian, and among the desert folk this is especially marked. Dinner followed not long after, a few large trays laid on the sand inside the tent, as it was now cold. We clustered round it and ate mainly in silence as it is polite to do. After most of us had eaten I tried the old bedouin joke, 'Where is the wind blowing from?' My friends looked at the pile of rice to see which side had been eaten away the quickest; just as the wind hollows out the sands, so do the eaters hollow out the rice. 'From the west,' they all murmured in agreement and pointed laughingly westward to fat Sultan who, as usual, had dug the deepest.

After dinner, coffee and tea followed one another as often as we felt inclined. Some of the bedouin would then tell stories. The shaikh would be asked questions on tribal politics or on any subject that occurred to his companions. If so prompted, he would then hold forth at length giving a considered view on the question raised using simple flowing language, sometimes quoting the Quran and sometimes the bedouin heroic poems. When this is done there will be a chorus of voices finishing the verse and adding others. Then one of our number would recite a new poem he had composed and memorized. The whole goes with a beautiful rhythm, and in describing this scene one gropes in vain for epithets; these occasions have a flavour that is unique. The more serious moments were always interspersed with joking and laughter.

In due course, the conversation would become less general. I would have a private chat with my neighbour and there would be some long silences. Silence amongst such a group may be lengthy, and it is perfectly acceptable in bedouin society. Eventually, when I thought a suitable moment had come to take my leave and to wish my hosts a good night, or rather, in the Arab phrase, 'A happy arising in the morning', I would retire to my tent.

Even in winter, when tents are a comfort if you are not to suffer from the piercing cold of the desert at night, there is a wonderful freedom about the desert camp. One particular joy to me is that there is no noise that is unattractive. There are the low murmur of voices, the crackle of a thorn fire, the clinking of the coffee mortar, a cry to a companion to fetch something. Above us all, the stars are clear and bright, and the surrounding spaces are so still, so wide. I slept well on such nights.

The Company had six concessions in the Trucial States and so I had six Rulers to visit. This aspect of my work was always a particular pleasure, the only trial being that the Company's survey work seldom stretched at any time over more than one or two shaikhdoms. Everyone was impatient, naturally, for the work to proceed faster and we all longed for results.

3

The Tribal Structure

There are many different types of tribe in Arabia. They vary from the totally sedentary to the totally nomadic, and there are very many which are at some point in between these two extremes. They vary likewise in size and in the complexity of their organization; but they have all developed on the same kind of pattern. Details change, the pattern remains. One tribe may, for example, join up with others under a strong leadership. Another tribe may be dividing into its constituent parts because of the absence of a strong personality. They do not lose their identity when these changes are made, or at least not for very many years.

The tribal pattern which can still be seen today has, above all, the characteristics of an Islamic society, and one that has existed with some gradual changes perhaps, but in its essence without change of principle, since the earliest days of Islam. There is evidence that many characteristics of tribal organization pre-date Islam. Even the language has hardly changed and I believe that a present-day tribesman from the desert, transported back over a thousand years to a similar tribal situation, would be able to carry on a conversation without any difficulty as to either substance or language. The only variations in language are dialectical differences between tribes, but some tribes in Southern Arabia have their own ancient language.

The most important feature of the tribe is kinship (*asabiyah*). It is the kinship and close intermarriage within the main families which gives the tribe its cohesiveness. Here there is an apparent paradox: the bedouin in particular is noted for his feeling of total freedom and independence. No one gives him orders, yet the tribe depends on cohesiveness without which they must perish. The tribesmen are dependent on one another in their ceaseless struggle with the harsh environment and their need for defence against any enemies. The tribe would succumb to both these dangers were it not for the spirit of the tribesman which constantly reminds him that the good of the whole tribe comes before his own immediate interest. He must sacrifice himself at any moment for the sake of his neighbours in the tribe. Here not only kinship but the spirit of selflessness, chivalry, readiness to self-sacrifice, which is called *muruwah*, is the key. This is a difficult word to translate as it has all the meanings attached to the idea of honour, nobility of spirit or, perhaps best, of chivalry; it demands the highest ideals and yet at the same time it is the minimum requirement. This ideal spirit can be found under very good leadership, when it may pervade the tribe and not simply be the attribute of the best tribesmen only, as it might be in a very poorly led tribe. Then poorly led tribes usually contrive a change of leader before long.

The key to the choice of leadership is the affirmation of allegiance (*mubayah*). The exact nature of the act of affirmation may differ slightly, but generally a group of elders chooses the new leader, and then the people are gathered together and the new shaikh, who is usually from the principal shaikhly family, is acclaimed and allegiance pledged publicly. It is interesting that the chroniclers of the history of Oman describe this in detail, and although it is an Ibadhi state, the requirements are in many ways like those of the ideal Sunni state as they were in the days of the early Califate or an idealized Califate, as described by Ibn Khaldun in the fourteenth century.

In a truly tribal society where there is little or no central government influence, a shaikh is alone at the top of the structure; but he would be warned by senior responsible tribesmen if his decisions were proving unacceptable. It might be made clear to him that his decision, unsupported, would not be considered binding. He would be pressured to accept advice before pronouncing. If all this failed a new man would be elected. The replacement might sometimes involve violence but more often not. The leader's duties in all tribes are the upholding of religion, attending the Friday prayer, the question of deciding matters of defence, of war and peace, the punishment of wrongdoers, the administration of justice, the collection of taxes (especially the religious tax), the administration of funds and personal supervision of all the community's affairs. This varies in detail according to the size and importance of the tribe and its capacities. In a small tribe cut off in the desert, divided into even smaller sections, the shaikh or the head of section or the head of family assumes the responsibility for justice, especially when it is simply not practical to go to a qualified *qadi* or judge, and the tribe could not afford to appoint one anyway.

I have seen many examples of the nomadic tribe, when near a settled area, referring its cases to the judge of the settled tribe nearest to them. The shaikh or junior leader, if his section is isolated, lives very much in public and has to make convincingly good decisions on each case in serious matters involving peace or war. Taking counsel (*shura*) from the elders or from those who happen to be with him at the time is essential, and reaching a consensus (and often working his companions' feelings towards a consensus) is the required method. As I understand it, the good shaikh will acquire a reputation for sound judgement and for knowing the probable consensus in advance, so that with time his decisions become more and more accepted, as he becomes the acknowledged authority with less and less need to ask for advice. As long as he can keep this up his authority will grow; but he must always be prepared to hear advice and criticism. The leader who does not take advice or who makes bad decisions may be lawfully deposed, either by the tribe as a whole, or by the elders, usually the people of the main family. Then someone will be put in his place; I have seen this happen.

In a nomadic tribe in particular, the leading shaikh – who is usually called the paramount or the *Tamima* – has to be assisted by other shaikhs who lead sections of the tribe and they, in their turn, by leaders of sub-sections and even family heads. A nomadic tribe, whether large or small, may be dispersed over an enormous area. A tribe such as the Manasir is found in Abu Dhabi on land and at sea and, at the same time, sections of it may be outside the Emirate. This particular tribe's economy depended upon camel breeding in the sand-dune areas of the Baynunah or on the northern edges of the Empty Quarter, and on date palms in the Liwa, as well as on pearl diving in the Gulf itself. That such a tribe can remain a cohesive whole is a proof of the strength of the tribal feeling of unity. Although today all the tribe is directly under one shaikh, the Emir Zayed, in the past it was accustomed to be under three main but quite separate shaikhs, one in charge of each of the main sections, with each sub-section controlled by lesser shaikhs, who would be found in all the various regions where the tribesmen plied their lawful occasions which would themselves be seasonal. The tribe as a whole was, however, under the Abu Dhabi shaikhs. The simple tribal structure would in such cases be flexible enough to keep the tribal entity together even when it was so divided by the complexities of the tribesmen's ways of earning their livelihood.

An essential feature of the position of all these shaikhs is that they are no more than *primus inter pares* but are nevertheless given great respect and clearly their prominence and authority depend upon their personality, their skill in leadership and on their ability to administer the Sharia law and the tribal custom. During my years in the Arab world I have had the good fortune on many occasions to observe shaikhs in the management of their tribes and thus to see the differing techniques which they apply in accordance with their varied personalities and the differing circumstances of the tribe in question. There is no doubt that there is something very glamorous about a really effective tribal leader: he is on his own; he has no bureaucracy to support him; he may or may not have recourse to a *qadi* for the trickier religious and legal problems which he has to face; he is himself on trial every minute of every day because his people have chosen him and will only continue to support him if he measures up to their requirements.

The *majlis*, be it a tent or the shade of a tree on the edge of the desert, wherever the shaikh and his people may be sitting, is very revealing to anyone who has seen a number of such gatherings. The shaikh and his companions have a very close identity of interest and they share the expertise which is necessary for their kind of life. The skills which nomads need and which all normal tribesmen will acquire to a greater or lesser extent, are remarkable to us and, until the new way of life of the oil revolution came to them so recently, every single man of the tribe would to us seem a great expert. The shaikh, if he is to lead effectively, must be at least as good as the average, and better than most, in all the different forms of expertise.

To begin with, his knowledge of the area of his tribal ranging ground (*dar* or *dira*) will be infinitely detailed. To a nomad, events do not happen near a place, they happen at a place, because every bit of the desert or the steppe country in which they live has a name to itself. In the Gulf the same can be said of the sea and every pearl bed, of which there are many hundreds, every submerged sandbank, every rock, has its name. The tribe has no veterinary surgeon: every tribesman is his own and, although some are better than others, all will cope. When you remember that their lives are dependent on the good health of their animals, this is something which matters. Individuals may be expert trackers, but all bedouin are trackers, and many is the time we have come upon camel tracks in sand which looked to me no more than saucer-shaped dents in the surface and the bedouin will look at them and say, 'Oh, that's so-and-so bin so-and-so who came past here yesterday afternoon and his camel is laden and he is going to such and such a place; he came by ten days ago going the other way with two camels and a saluki dog. He said he would be coming back in a few days. His big camel would be heavily laden with goods for his family and for some others. The smaller camel he would ride and it would be less heavily laden. Here are the dog's tracks at the side. Here are the deep tracks of the heavily laden camel. Now his riding camel I know well as I have had it with me when taking camels out grazing and guarding them. I would know its tracks anywhere, see these rather small feet and the stride is long for so small a camel, but then it is very fast . . .' and so he will go on. It is all very easy: if you have studied tracks all your life you can interpret them as easily as a reader reads a book.

I have seen a senior shaikh himself dosing a camel or skilfully splicing a broken feather on the wing of a hawk. Hunting was not just a sport, it was a necessity of life; even now, hunting trips are still, as they always were, one of the many ways an effective shaikh can use to keep in touch with his people. Such a shaikh is still forever doing what his people do and, as far as he can, doing it at least as well, and often much better. Plainly a shaikh with a big personality establishes this in the minds of his companions and after a few years his position may be easier for him to build upon, but he must be constantly under strain since the better he is, the higher the expectation of his wisdom. I have watched shaikhs when they were on the point of establishing their fame and others long after they had achieved it, and it is not difficult to see the constant exertion required to maintain their leadership.

One particular Omani shaikh of an almost wholly sedentary tribe invited me to stay with him for a week and wanted me to observe how he carried on the management of the tribe. This was ten years ago, when the insidious bureaucracy was already creeping into his area. His overlord, the Sultan of Oman, had wisely decided to give him freedom to use his own authority to help direct his people towards the unwonted ways of the bureaucrate and act as a liaison – almost a lubricant – in their relationship with the central government authority. It was an exacting week because his *majlis* was my bedroom and it was only mine from midnight to six in the morning; at other times it was thronged with visitors. People came to see him one after another all through the day and we had many guests to every meal. When he went out, people would be at the crossroads to stop his car and ask him for help and in the villages there would be a place in the market for him to sit where people would be gathered already awaiting him.

This particular shaikh stopped many cases going before the courts by persuading the participants to accept his judgement. Here was a shaikh of the twentieth century reduced officially to the status of a welfare officer or counsellor in legal cases, but the fact that he was still accepted – and indeed preferred in so many cases to the official courts – showed that he carried forward the mantle which dates back hundreds of years. Although he would sometimes take over cases and decide them out of court, as the courts of the central government had been established in the area this tribal duty had gradually waned. Many cases he dealt with by referring to the appropriate official to whom he would speak on the telephone or perhaps send a written message. What I was witnessing was the end of tribalism and the beginning of bureaucracy and it seemed to me that the central government and the shaikh were handling the change with great dexterity.

This change has been going on all over Eastern Arabia. Whereas thirty years ago each little oasis or port was run on a tribal pattern, similar to that of the bedouin, they are now being absorbed into the organizations of the central government – the bedouin being left to the last. This is probably an acceleration of a process which has been going on for hundreds of years at a much slower rate. There has been a tendency for bedouin to come into the settled areas, perhaps over a very long time, and it is interesting that in most settled areas of Eastern Arabia it is the shaikhs of the senior bedouin families who provide the aristocracy.

The introduction of modern weapons and aircraft has created a change in the position of the bedouin tribes. Sixty or seventy years ago the bedouin had complete control in the desert, and in Oman this was certainly the case up to 1954. Central governments had no control in the desert and had to negotiate with the bedouin over questions such as the access of caravans and the use of the desert. This is no longer the case.

Many tribes which habitually crossed frontiers, especially in and out of Iraq, Jordan, Syria, Saudi Arabia and Oman, would accept the ruling of the local court, and pay the religious tax to the officials of whichever country they just happened to be in or passing through. During the international arbitration over the Saudi/Abu Dhabi boundary, this question of tax collecting was disputed. One side said that collection of religious tax (*zakat*) by an official of a country from a traveller meant that the traveller was a subject of the country which collected the tax. The opposing view was that taxing of nomadic tribesmen had no bearing either on the nationality of the payer or sovereignty over the ground where the payment happened to be made. The conclusion I drew was that there was no notion in Eastern Arabia of frontiers in the grazing areas of nomads until oil companies came along and wanted a political dividing line on the ground between neighbouring countries, and payment of *zakat* did not have the same political significance as in settled areas.

If you look at a tribe as if it were a city state, and I think the analogy is helpful, then a nomadic tribe would be seen as a mobile city state. If this tribe does not have much by way of an administration then it will make use of the administrators of whatever Muslim state happens to be nearest at the time. Modern conceptions of the need for frontiers to ascertain mineral and other rights upset this arrangement.

Historically the concept of the tribal area is important. The range may be in a few cases totally exclusive, the tribe allowing absolutely no person from other tribes to cross it, but total exclusivity is not common. In Oman, the Duru and Al Bu Shams exercised such exclusion successfully. More common was partial exclusivity, whereby permission to enter a tribe's ground might be sought and granted. I remember in the early fifties during a period of drought in al-Hasa in Saudi Arabia, a few of the al-Murra tribe came over to Abu Dhabi and were granted permission by the Ruler to graze their camels for the winter in the Abu Dhabi deserts where there had been more rain than in Eastern Saudi Arabia that year. Had the grazing in Abu Dhabi been quite inadequate, the Ruler would have had the right to refuse, but this would have been a very difficult decision to make.

Many characteristics of tribal organization are of particular interest. Notable among them is the *Rafiq* or Companion system. This is usually employed to help a visitor from another tribe or a total stranger. The *Rafiq* concerned accepts the visitor as if he were a member of his tribe, and once he has done this he is answerable for his safety. When travelling within his own tribal area the arrangement thus makes the visitor an honorary member of the tribe. When travelling in another tribe's area this may even be a stronger bond. Assuming that the two tribes are at peace, were anything to happen to the stranger in the second tribe's territory while the *Rafiq* position is operative, the death or injury of the stranger would be a terrible disgrace to the tribe of the *Rafiq*. It could start a war between the two tribes.

A most important and interesting feature of all tribal life, not just that of the bedouin, is the *wasm* or brand mark used to show the tribal ownership of animals. This is made up of lines, dots and half circles and is burnt into the skin at a particular place. It might be on the neck or on a thigh or a leg. Within the tribe animals would be known, although some tribes have a difference in the brand for the various sections. Brands are needed to claim an animal which has strayed away from the tribe or has been stolen. These brands are the best evidence in tracing tribal history and descent.

The tribesmen have a keen sense of their own history and this is recorded in their narrative heroic poems, which trace and record the main events of tribal history. When one checks these against other sources, the accuracy and detail are very impressive, although in the case of quarrels the poet might be prejudiced in favour of his side. The only omission is a direct form of dating. Some of the poetry is not always strictly narrative in form, but is purely poetical, as are many of the songs. Fortunately belated steps are now being taken in several countries to commit this traditional material to paper. Owing to the change in lifestyle, the evening sittings of a tribe or part of a tribe round the fire no longer happen in the way they did, certainly not on the same scale nor with the same regularity, so that the custom of reciting and memorizing poetry is in danger, before long, of dying.

I discussed some of the main points I have made here with a wise and delightful paramount shaikh of an important tribe that used to be one of the most wholly nomadic. 'But,' he said, 'you have missed the main point about the good shaikh.' 'What is that?' 'He must have *hadh*' (good fortune). 'With *hadh* you can lead, you can make peace not war, the good shaikh makes peace.' 'And without *hadh*?' 'Without *hadh* you would not be the shaikh!'

All this points to the tribes having developed a system of self-rule over the centuries. This works in a similar way in the case of big and small tribes, but the system tends to be influenced by central government in the case of settled tribes whenever settled government becomes strong in the tribal area. In recent years changes in lifestyle and the invasion of the desert by the motor car and the aeroplane are likewise having their impact on bedouin tribes.

The salient feature, and the most interesting one in my view, is the stability and longevity of the tribal system. Although tribal history contains stories of fights and raids, stability and peaceful existence are really much more marked features of the tribes. Individual shaikhs often ruled for several decades and shaikhly families for centuries. The aim of the system was continuity and this was achieved.

4

The Background to the Search for Oil and My Involvement

Most people would agree if they look back that their careers are dictated more by events than by their inclinations. We may nudge the tiller from time to time and think we manage to set something of a new course, but events may prove otherwise. I think it was chance that set me reading books about Arabia when I was at Oxford in the last three years before World War II, chance and the fact that so many very readable books – some great literature – were written about this subject in English. I am thinking of such writers as Burton, Gertrude Bell, Doughty and perhaps even, with some reservations, T.E. Lawrence. There are many others.

I had just got my degree in modern history when war broke out. I tried to join up at once, as a private soldier, but they would not have me as I had passed an army exam during my service as a cadet with the Oxford Cavalry Squadron. I had to wait and was then pushed willynilly as a Second Lieutenant into the Royal Army Service Corps (RASC). I went to France, returning wet but in one piece via Dunkirk; then bored with Britain, I volunteered for service in the Middle East because of my interest in that area. I was sent in due course to Syria for the campaign against the Vichy French. Then came several stays in hospital where I met and made friends with officers of the newly formed airborne services, soon to be called SAS (Special Air Service), who offered a change from the RASC. They trained me as a parachutist and sent me back to Syria to work out how we could stay on in small parties if the Germans took Syria, as seemed so likely after the fall of Crete, and later because of advances by the Germans in the desert war. We could have done little to stop them coming in but we might have made life awkward for them. This assignment enabled me to travel on foot, camel or horse all over Syria, mountains and desert, and gave me the opportunity to study the hill people and the bedouin.

During part of my time in Syria I was working under the direction of Wilfred Thesiger, from whom I managed to learn a great deal about the Arab World (but he was annoyingly reticent about his exploits in Abyssinia for which he had been honoured with the DSO). Life with him was very interesting, enjoyable, and to say the least unusual. It was an education in itself. Then came a short spell in Iraq, which ended at my request, after which I was sent to the Western Desert of Egypt for the closing stages of the campaign in North Africa; lastly I joined the 7th Armoured Division, 'The Desert Rats', for the Salerno landing in Italy. When later the Division was pulled out of Italy we were sent to England to prepare for Normandy and thus I was back in action in France on D-Day, 6 June 1944. I stayed with the same Division right up to Hamburg in May 1945. After the war ended I soon became frustrated with the army of occupation as we were allowed no fraternization with the Germans and I had nothing much to do. While in Arabia I had come to know Glubb Pasha, the already famous leader of the Arab Legion, the army of Transjordan, who were then becoming involved in the campaign in Iraq against the revolutionary government who were in sympathy with the Nazis. A signal to him from me in Hamburg in due course resulted in a posting for me to the Arab Legion, on condition that I signed on for two years, rather than be demobilized in six months as would have happened otherwise. I then served for some time with bedouin troops in Palestine and Jordan. It was while I was with the Arab Legion that another event took place which was later to alter my life.

I was instructed to take charge as conducting officer of the Arab Legion contingent to take part in the May 1946 victory parade in London. It was a party of some forty Jordanian soldiers, led by a general and several other senior and junior officers, most of whom had no word of English, and only two junior officers and myself had enough of both languages to translate for us all. Among the more notable duties which we performed was the trooping of our colour at Windsor with the Household Cavalry regiment (as the two regiments of Horse Guards then still were) to commemorate the joint Arab Legion-British advance into Iraq in 1941.

In talk at the subsequent lunch at Windsor in the officers' mess it was arranged that the general, Abdul Qadir Pasha Jundi, would sit next to His Majesty King George VI in the royal enclosure at the Windsor horse-show that afternoon and I would have to interpret for him for however long the horse-show lasted. I was naturally rather nervous and felt my inadequacy, but there was no one else who could do it.

After we were settled in our places His Majesty made a rather complicated joke, quite amusingly told, about whether it was better to apply for a place at Eton for one's son or for a Ford car, as they were both in short supply. I explained to the general at some length that the story was too difficult for me to translate, but that it was amusing and when I stopped speaking, I said, would he please laugh? My predicament tickled him sufficiently to make him laugh heartily and the rest of the conversation went quite easily after that. The King's well-known stammer soon disappeared and things went smoothly. The general subsequently insisted that I always interpreted for him wherever we went, and at a lunch which was given by the Iraq Petroleum Company (an international oil company which had concessions in Jordan, Syria, Iraq and the lower Gulf), I seem to have impressed someone in the company enough to have a job offered to me when I left the army.

In 1947 while I was on leave from the Arab Legion I was suddenly posted back to the British Army in Haifa, despite Glubb Pasha's remonstrance, because the army had sudden need of an airborne major with my qualifications. So it was that I saw out the last nine months of the agony of the British Mandate in Palestine with the 6th Airborne in Haifa. Our last days in Haifa in 1948 were miserable, not so much because of the almost constant shooting every night, which endangered us all, but because we so clearly were handing over the city to the Jews, and almost all the Arab citizens were driven out by the Jewish irregular armies under our noses in not much over twenty-four hours on 21 and 22 April 1948. The Jews even complained to us on the 23rd that they were having difficulty in providing municipal services as the Arab municipal workers appeared 'strangely' to have left. The whole operation was completed without our being able to interfere. We were not permitted to move a finger to stop it. The view in regard to Palestine which I then held, and I have not seen reason to question it since, is that we should have offered the Jews and others released from the camps in Germany a place in the UK, and, to make this easier for ourselves, persuade or at least attempt to persuade the Americans and French to do the same in their countries. I felt sure we were wrong to give them a country already completely populated with Arabs who had been there since prehistoric days; the country was not ours to give away.

Thus, in August 1948 I was back in the UK, a civilian once more, and I took the oil company up on their offer of a job, having first failed to get into the Foreign Service. At the headquarters of the oil company in London, I was told that I was to start in October in the Arabian Gulf as company representative in Dubai for the Trucial States and I would have special responsibility in Muscat and Oman, where we hoped to begin exploration. We already held the concession.

Glad as I was to leave Palestine in those last terrible days, I was sorry that the exciting chapter with the Arab Legion had ended. From the generals down I had found them all delightful people to work with, full of good humour, always interesting, and above all friendly. Much as I had enjoyed the friendship and comradeship of the British army, there was something very fascinating about the Arab Legion, especially the evening *majlis* in a tent or in the open desert, when officers and men would sit together and with a frankness controlled only by the minimum amount of respect due to those in authority. Such frankness seemed only possible with British troops in smaller groups.

I accepted the idea of going to the Gulf gladly. I was happy not to have to hunt for work, and the prospect looked interesting. Pay would be modest, but living costs were mainly met by the company. It was a matter of following the line of least resistance and this turned out to be a choice I did not regret.

Reading about the area presented some difficulty since there were not many reliable books in print at that time on the Gulf countries, but I was helped by a friend in the Foreign Office who let me have some books which I would otherwise not have found easily. Historians love to argue as to whether the British presence was primarily in pursuit of trade or as a part of her strategic moves to defend India, in the first instance, and then the whole Empire which stretched beyond to the East as the second aim. By 1948 our direct responsibility for the defence of India no longer existed in the way in which it had preoccupied us for so long, but we thought of the subcontinent as vital to the Commonwealth and our relationship with both Pakistan and India as being something of very great importance to us, especially just after World War Two, in which the British owed so much to the armies raised in the Indian sub-continent. The Commonwealth link to Australia and to Malaya was still of importance to us, and both this and the possibilities of further oil discoveries in which companies, some at least partly British, were involved, made the region one of the very greatest importance in the eyes of Whitehall. We had come as traders but stayed for mercantile, strategic and, therefore, political reasons combined.

I was keen to see another part of the Arab world. I had enjoyed tremendously my work in Arab countries so far. An entirely new area, therefore, was very attractive to me. I had seen little of the townspeople in the Arab states of the Fertile Crescent; I had, however, seen much more of the country people and the bedouin. With the latter I had been taught by the precept of Wilfred Thesiger that if you were prepared to live exactly as they did, bringing in nothing extraneous, apart from yourself (a strange enough phenomenon to be going on with), they would gladly accept your presence with them. All this meant, however, relying on hospitality, impossible ever to repay. The country people in particular in the Fertile Crescent were lavish with their time, would stay with you all day, guide you to the next place, wanting nothing in return. The expression 'returning hospitality' which is so familiar to us would, I felt, seem an uncouth conception to them. My study of the bedouin in Syria and Jordan in the forties would, I hoped, be useful to me in the Gulf.

I was to go to Bahrain at the beginning of October 1948 to stay with Basil Lermitte, the Company's manager there, who was responsible for the relations with the various governments regarding work in all those countries of the Gulf in which the Company had concessions for the exploration and the development of oil. As far as I was concerned this meant the Trucial States and Oman. Basil Lermitte was renowned for his knowledge of the lower Gulf, where he had been for several years, travelling over the whole of the area more often by boat than by air. At the time I arrived the Company did not keep planes stationed in the Gulf, though they were planning to do so. Basil had done many trips in small boats and pioneered many desert crossings by car, and I looked forward to doing the same.

In 1947 when India became independent the Foreign Office in London assumed responsibility for the Gulf, and from then on British diplomats gradually took over the positions previously held by the Indian Political Service, retaining the old Indian titles of Political Officer, Political Agent and Political Resident (the last being the most senior). A Political Officer had been posted to Sharjah for the first time on a permanent basis in 1948 just before I arrived. In the Trucial States the company had just started its seismic programme in the search for oil. The

Trucial States were the shaikhdoms which were to become the United Arab Emirates in 1971. In those days they were separate shaikhdoms, each in Treaty Relations with Britain.

The problem in Oman was that although the Sultan, Saiyid Said bin Taimor, was the overall sovereign, a part of the interior, the highland area round the central massif of Jabal Akhdar, as well as the mountain area to the east, was under an Ibadhi Imam. In 1921 an agreement had been signed between the government of Oman in Muscat and some of the leading shaikhs of the interior, whereby the senior tribal shaikhs were granted considerable freedom, and in effect something approaching autonomy in all local affairs. The Imam was not named in this document. The Sultan of course did not wish to imply recognition of his office as Imam. However, the central highland area of Oman was ruled by the 'Imam' Muhammad bin Abdullah and the leaders of the two tribal factions the Hinawi and Ghafiri groups. In Oman the Ibadhi state was traditionally headed by an Imam, and to recognize him as Imam would imply he was the sovereign in the state, rather than the Sultan himself. This agreement, known as the Agreement of Sib (a place on the coast north-west of Muscat) represented a difficulty for our company.

Our concession to search for oil was with the Sultan, as the sovereign power, alone. It was his responsibility to enable our prospecting parties to go into the interior to search for oil. The difficulty of previous years had been that the shaikhs of the interior, whether under the Imam's own aegis in the Jabal Akhdar area or in the separate region to the north near al-Buraimi (in the Dhahirah plain), claimed that they also had a right to receive money from the Company if it was to explore on their territory. The Sultan would allow no substantial payments to be made which might be construed later as proving that the oil in the area concerned belonged to the shaikhs and not to him. So far he had not been able to deliver his part of the bargain and thus gain access for the Company into the interior. From a legal point of view his attitude seemed right, but the question remained as to whether he could deliver politically.

In the winter of 1948–9 the Sultan had promised all would be well. We should begin in the Dhahirah region where the shaikhs of the three big tribes, the Bani Kaab, the Al Bu Shams and the Naim, had agreed to the paramountcy of Shaikh Saqr al-Naimi, the Shaikh of Buraimi, who would, the Sultan said, guarantee our entry, without our making any special payment.

Dick Bird, the senior official from London who was to lead us, was to arrive in a few weeks. He and I would go to Buraimi to ensure that all was well, and if we thought it was, then we would call for the geologists, who were still working in Iraq and Qatar on the Company's fields. When the geologists came we would all go down together to Muscat and then go back into the interior on a track which the Sultan claimed he had opened up. It was in a valley called the Wadi al-Jizzi. He wanted us to do the whole operation on Sultanate territory. It all looked nice and easy but one wondered, with the history of the immediate past, what would happen on the ground. Dick intended to base the expedition at first on the Abu Dhabi side where we knew we would be welcome to stay, but before the geologists could start work we would have to enter the area from Oman. In the early summer when the geologists would leave I was to take over the post in Dubai of Jackson, who was the Company representative to the Trucial States, with continuing responsibilities in Oman.

I spent three or four days in Bahrain, happily meeting new people and hearing about the nature of our work. On the Trucial Coast I could see that an early task would be to get to know all the shaikhs of the different shaikhdoms whose capitals were distributed along the 160 miles or so of coast. Some of them were to be found more often fifty or more miles inland at their various oases. This does not sound far, but some of these journeys were much more arduous than they look on the map, involving as they did crossing the high sands of virgin desert and, on the coasts, wide areas of treacherous mud-flats; I thought that my experience of the Western Desert of Egypt might be a help.

Basil Lermitte took me with him on an official visit to the Ruler of Bahrain, His Highness Shaikh Salman, a charming and dignified man with whom we conversed in Arabic, and inevitably I found myself encouraged to do most of the talking. This was Basil's habit. I was a bit afraid that my Arabic would seem strange as it was then a mixture of a rather superficial classical, Syrian and Egyptian. The last two dialects do not go well together but a modicum of classical provides the necessary lubricant. If I were to start learning Arabic again I would stick more closely to the classical which is the passport to anywhere in Arabia.

Shaikh Salman was interested in what I had to say about the Levant, and he did not surprise me by being very critical of much of HMG's policy over Israel. However, he was very restrained and polite in the way he phrased his criticism, and this, I was told, was always his nature.

On the following day I was to get up early to catch an RAF plane, the weekly 'milk-run' to Sharjah on the Trucial coast. The Company had close links with the RAF, who allowed civilians to buy a ticket for their Gulf runs provided there was empty space. Bahrain airport was a small single-storey building and its runway, which had been developed during World War II for allied airforces, was long enough for the largest planes but was made of the perforated steel plates which had been used in the war in Normandy and elsewhere for emergency strips. These were simply laid on to the rolled salt-flat and while they were serviceable enough for a time they tended to curl up at the ends and would become dangerous if they were not constantly attended to. Our heavily laden Dakota with few passengers and much in the way of stores and equipment lumbered into the air after a bumpy ride down the strip. We flew directly to Sharjah, passing over a few islands on the way, and during the flight I gazed down at the blue sea and turned over in my mind what I had been told in London in very broad terms, and in Bahrain in more detail, my work would be.

I was looking forward to the expedition into the Omani desert, and I was to help Jackson in Dubai in setting up the necessary transport and equipment for the expedition, and then join it myself. Dubai would be our base for our work inland. It was with some excitement that, after two hours' flight in the slow-moving Dakota, I saw in the distance the low sandy shore. As we came in to land I could see over on our right a small town which I took to be Dubai clustered round a creek, and as we circled I looked down on a small and rather rudimentary airstrip beside which were a few low buildings, the most considerable being in the shape of a *Beau Geste* fort. A little way behind it was Sharjah, in those days a very small town, and beyond it the sea. The town was in a desert setting which stretched as far as one could see inland in all directions. There were no other aircraft on the ground and our arrival was something of an occasion since scheduled planes came in only once a week. There were no customs formalities and no one seemed interested in passports. The sun was setting, there was a gentle breeze from the sea, humid and sticky. Inland one could see nothing but low dunes. I was excited and wanted to see this place I had heard so much about. It was to be my home for an unknown number of years, and at first appearance it seemed quite different, in some indefinable way, from anywhere I had been to before despite my familiarity with desert scenes.

As soon as I got out of the plane I was met by Jackson, or Jacko, as he was known. He was to prove a cheerful companion, scholarly and somewhat academic in approach, and a fluent Arabic speaker. We went in a Humber pick-up round the end of Dubai creek itself, a ride of forty-five minutes, travelling at speed in the darkness over the salt-flats but at a more leisurely pace over switch-back dunes where the fat sand tyres bore us confidently and all was well provided we did not stop or go too slowly. It was October, still warm and sticky, but pleasant enough at night, and we came to a halt by a two-storey house overlooking the creek whose façade was broken by a series of white Moorish arches which fronted a long wide verandah on the first floor. Jacko explained that the house was all the Company had in Dubai; the end room was his office; there were three bedrooms and a sitting room and that was all it amounted to. He said that the Ruler of Dubai, Shaikh Said bin Maktum, was very friendly and helpful, as indeed were all the shaikhs; there were five other rulers with whom we had concessions and I must call on them, if time allowed to get to know them before I was to go into the interior. Of the six rulers, especially important were the shaikhs of Abu Dhabi whom I would meet in due course.

Leaning over the verandah railings we could see much of the town in the strong moonlight. Nearby were two-storey houses like ours, fronting the creek and made from mud and coral with wooden beams. Beyond were hundreds of brown palm-reed huts called *barastis*. Most of Dubai was then built in this way. The creek in front of us was swiftly flowing with the incoming tide and perhaps two hundred yards in width. Between us and the sea it serpentined first to our left and then back to the right to turn once again to a sand bar where it met the open sea. Small rowing boats, some carrying lanterns, plied quietly up and down like the sampans of the Far East, and these boats were the normal form of transport inside the town. The twin towns of Dubai and Deira lay on either side of the creek, and I was told that once feuding had caused a fight which was waged across the narrow water; but all was quiet now under the control of old Shaikh Said and his son, Rashid.

I had a few days to become acclimatized before starting to check the preparations for the forthcoming expedition. Jacko had in any case got most things ready: piles of tins of bully-beef and tinned vegetables, cans of petrol and four sturdy Chevrolet pick-ups with a team of drivers led by

Firdullah bin Khairallah and Sabir bin Muhammad, Dick Bird's drivers of the season before.

Over the next week Sabir took me to see some of the shaikhs and taught me something of his technique of sand driving in cars which had power only on the back wheels. To make up for lack of four-wheel drive we had wide, low-pressure tyres and carried tin sand-channels to put under the wheels when they were stuck; but try as I would, I could never equal the excellence of either Firdullah or Sabir as sand drivers.

The area of the Trucial States was still subject to feuding, and there was no police and no army. Order was maintained by the armed followers of the shaikhs. Not so long before there had been fighting between Dubai and Sharjah. Ancient muzzle-loading cannon would 'exchange shots'. In this case it was literally true, since the bedouin could sometimes recover the enemy's shots and fire them back at him.

While this war continued, Imperial Airways, the forerunner of BOAC, would still refuel their flying-boats on Dubai creek and send the passengers over to the fort in Sharjah by bus for lunch. During this operation the war was suspended by mutual agreement between the belligerents, and passengers would pass through the 'lines' without, in most cases, realizing anything unusual was afoot, since the air crews, who knew about it, had no wish to alarm them by explaining it. By the time I arrived, this little war was over and there were no longer any flying-boats alighting on Dubai creek.

None of the men of Dubai would ever go out of town unarmed since attacks on camel convoys, or even cars, by bedouin were always a possibility. We, on the other hand, were never armed and seldom took guards with us, as we were never attacked when they realized who we were. As guests living under the protection of the shaikhs we were safe, and if ever the shaikhs thought it necessary for a particular journey they would give us guards. The only areas where we encountered difficulties were on the borders between Oman and the shaikhdoms and in Oman itself.

The friendly co-operation of the people of the shaikhdoms made life very easy and comfortable. The one cause for disquiet to me was the absence of any state revenues in any of these territories to relieve the poverty of the people. The standard of living was low, little above subsistence level. Nevertheless people seemed tolerably happy and cheerful, and, in a land where hardly anyone was rich, there was no room for jealousy. Medical care was not available in any modern form in those days, outside Dubai, and it was sketchy enough even there. Lack of refrigeration ruled out most modern medicines. Everyone, however, lived in the same sort of style and the poor were frequent guests at their Rulers' tables. The little the Rulers had, they would give away in hospitality and as presents to their people.

Not unnaturally from these very early days in the country the thought which was constantly in one's mind was what will happen to these people if no oil is found? Their way of life, relying as it did on pearling, was now becoming impossible; oil must be found. Such thoughts could never be far away from one's consciousness from then onwards.

5

The Search Begins

On our trip we were to take with us a radio set which would link us on speech to Jacko in Dubai and, through Dubai, with the Company office in Bahrain on key. Jacko had already sent a quantity of petrol by camel to al-Ain. This was the principal village in the Abu Dhabi sector in the group of oases of which the main Omani village was Buraimi. In those days in Dubai, petrol was still only available in the square, flimsy 'non-returnable' four-gallon tins of the war days, and each camel could take four of these in specially made wooden saddle boxes. Unfortunately, about one in four of these tins would prove to be a leaker, and would finish the journey partly or even wholly empty. Thus, although we had sent over a thousand tins in this way to the store which Dick Bird, who had just joined us from London, had built in al-Ain, it was a matter of chance as to how much had arrived.

One bright November afternoon in 1948 we set off in four two-wheel drive Chevrolet pick-ups. The whole journey, as the crow flies, was only a matter of 120 miles or so, but to get through the sands we had to travel first almost to Abu Dhabi town, on its island off the coast, and then strike inland. In those days there was not even a graded track to Abu Dhabi and you followed the tyre marks of predecessors or launched out afresh on to virgin desert as the mood took you. It was essential to watch the texture of the *sabkhas*, the salt-flats, to detect whether they were firm or soft. Rain, dew or a high tide could make them treacherous, and in the wet it was safer to follow earlier tracks through standing water, since where water stood the ground was firmer. We had tow-ropes, jacks, our sand channels and the know-how of our drivers to get us through. On that particular day it was a good and easy journey as far as the Abu Dhabi turn. There had been no rain and no recent high tides; the temperature was exactly right and all went well. We reached the Abu Dhabi-al-Ain track in two and a half hours. Then we turned inland and, heavily laden as we were, one of the cars got stuck crossing the first line of dunes. We stopped the other two on downward slopes, and all of us lent a hand. By dint of scooping away sand, lowering tyre pressures, pushing and using our sand channels, we got the truck going. By nightfall we reached a group of palm trees at the beginning of the massive pink sands and a well called Bidat al-Ajam (Well of the Persian). This was our objective and there we camped. This process involved merely getting out our bedding, making tea and opening a few tins for dinner. Previous expeditions had found that tents were, for the most part, not essential since it so seldom rained. I found this reasonable enough except in the very coldest weather inland, when a tent is a comfort at night, and for the next few years much of my time was spent in the open. I also preferred an air mattress to a camp bed, as the latter is unuseable in soft sand, the only snag being that you may be closer to any snakes and scorpions. On the few occasions when we took tents, we usually regretted it because their extra weight meant that we could take that much less petrol or water. We set up the radio and got in touch with Jacko at nine o'clock as we had previously agreed. Speech was not very clear, but we were in contact. We needed this to report our progress and the likelihood of our being ready to ask the geologists to join us.

Our plan was to wake early and, taking advantage of the dew-sodden, cool sands, get through the two lines of heavy sands which guard the approaches to al-Ain at sunrise. At about 5 a.m., just before sunrise, the first flies had us properly awake, and after a cup of tea, we loaded up and got on our way. We made good progress from Bidat al-Ajam over a mass of packed sand about five miles in extent. On either side rose hills of dunes with sharp crescent edges, their slip faces pointing southeast, and as we looked back at them, they glinted pink and yellow in the morning sun. The air was clear and cool; it was good to be alive and I was excited to see what lay ahead.

The next range of dunes was easily negotiated where they fall away leaving a gap at Bu Samra well. Above the well is a huge dune. The experts say dunes cannot lie at an angle steeper than 32° on the slip face, but this one always looks like a small mountain and, whether you only look at it or try to climb it, it seems much steeper than that. We stopped at the well and exchanged greetings with the bedouin we found sitting there. Sabir made us all Arab coffee while we began asking about the movements of the tribes in the area. Was Shaikh so-and-so at home? Where were his men? The bedouin were from the Awamir tribe, lean and tough. Their leader wore no headcloth as is the way of some of the bedouin of the high sands, but he had a thin head-rope of plaited leather tangled in his long black hair. Like the others, he wore a long coffee-coloured shirt, or *thawb*, that reached down to his ankles and carried an ancient Mauser rifle, a camel stick and a piece of light cane about three feet long with a slightly curved handle. He spoke in a deep, thick voice in short phrases and the liquid accent of the sands with long pauses between sentences.

First it was: 'No news. Praise be to God.' And, then at length, he told us of the latest episode in the twelve-year-old feud between his tribe and the Duru, the prospects of some settlement, the coming of their own Shaikh, Salim bin Hamm, and the possibility that Shaikh Zayed, brother of the Ruler of Abu Dhabi, might intervene. The feud had begun, according to the bedouin, with a theft of Awamir camels by some Duru several years earlier, at which time two herdsmen of the Awamir had been killed. Since then, at long intervals, other incidents had taken place: camel thefts or very occasionally killing. To us it sounded as if the Awamir were up on the score and might agree to make peace, but we had yet to hear the other side.

Although we had no immediate prospects of getting into Duru country, this was our ultimate objective; the most promising surface signs, geologically, of a possible oil-bearing formation, as we knew from our aerial reconnaissance, were in the middle of the desert which the Duru claimed as their own. The Duru were the Sultan of Oman's people, but so remote were they from Muscat that the Sultan could only be in contact with them at certain times. The Awamir were a tribe which originated in the Dakaka of the Eastern Aden Protectorate and roamed the territories of the Saudis, the Aden Protectorate, Abu Dhabi and the Sultanate alike. They would even be found, in some years, as far north as Kuwait and Iraq. An important section of the tribe had been living for years in Abu Dhabi, using al-Ain as their base. They were regarded as Abu Dhabi subjects.

The most interesting news for us was that Shaikh Zayed, the brother of the Ruler of Abu Dhabi and his governor in al-Ain, was away on a hunting trip to the south but expected back any day. Since he was by far the leading personality in the area, he was the key source for information in the whole region as to the doings of the tribes. The sun was now higher, and we wanted to cross the next and last chain of dunes before the sands had really dried out. The crossing point was the Haza al-Baush, a place that had become notorious for trapping cars in the soft sand. We crossed a bumpy bush-covered plain and could see in front of us the mass of the dune chain, and below one of its highest peaks was an obvious pass. As we approached we could see that the tracks of previous cars which came in from either side converged at one point opposite the col to be lost in the soft sand, and Dick drove flat out for this point. It felt as if we were airborne for half a minute, then the dunes were coming at us fast as we mounted a broad incline, rutted with car tracks, and once over the brow, we turned sharp right into a deep defile with a smooth mud-flat bottom.

Across the mud-flat stretched one ridge of sand and this had to be taken at about thirty miles an hour to give enough speed to race across another short mud-flat for the hard climb over the last and biggest dune. On this occasion he timed it just right and we cleared the ridge, wheels in the air, landed on the flat, accelerated, changed quickly down and charged the steep red dune that seemed to tower in front of us. We could feel the soft sand gripping and sucking at our tyres as our speed fell off; another quick gear change and we just breasted the crest to have before us a totally new scene: no more high dunes but level sand with trees and scrub and, beyond, the dark, sombre crags and cliffs of the mountain, Jebel Hafit, which hangs over al-Ain village and the whole oasis.

Later, in the hot weather of the following June, I found how much more difficult it could be when we were almost twenty-four hours in the Haza al-Baush with two new and recalcitrant trucks whose track rods would not take the strain but bent under the sand pressure. Firdullah and Sabir cheerfully took the track rods off, heated them up over a primus and straightened them. On that occasion Shaikh Zayed, who was camping in the neighbourhood, came over in his Chevrolet truck and we all had lunch together. It was the longest 'sticking' I remember, and we never took those particular trucks into the high dunes again.

Today the journey is done on a wide dual-carriageway tarmac road built above the sands. By what seems to me to be some kind of optical illusion, the dunes have now diminished in size as seen from a passing car and are not so impressive as when you are among them, since they are dwarfed by the road. But let anyone leave the road and try the dunes at another point, and he will see the sands as we used to see them and experience both their strange beauty and the problem they set as an obstacle.

We found our way along an easy sandy track among the acacia trees into the oasis. This was a group of nine separate villages, three in Muscat territory and six in Abu Dhabi. Each village consisted of a cluster of low mud-brick houses set in large date groves, and in between the villages was open scrub. To the north was a small forest of acacia and other thorn trees; to the south were two gaunt ribs of Jebel Hafit and the main mass of the mountain which shuts in the oasis. There were several further palm groves on the Abu Dhabi side.

We made straight for the fort of Jahili. This was a mud-brick fortress with two large quadrangles set in high walls with corner towers and near the centre a robust but battered round turret, all of sun-dried clay brick. It was built by Shaikh Zayed's famous grandfather, Shaikh Zayed bin Khalifah, towards the end of last century, but the underground channel, called a *falaj*, which served it with water from a spring some three miles away, had 'died', in the local phrase, and the gardens had died with it, so that the fort had been abandoned and was partly in ruins. But it had a few sound rooms remaining, and these had been allocated to Dick by Shaikh Zayed to use as he liked whenever he wanted.

We reached Fort Jahili and found it empty and forlorn. The rooms were bare, their floors of sand, and the windows unshuttered and without glass. This was to be our home for some months to come. We had brought no furniture other than rugs, but by the time we had laid them out, together with our bedding rolls, the place began to look more like home. Our rolled-up blankets with rugs over them formed useful cushions to lean on as we sat. In another building, we set up the radio with its poles outside, and in another we made a kitchen. It was real luxury. The one snag was the courtyard which was of loose sand, and every now and again a small whirlwind would cross it to blow the sand in clouds into our rooms. But this was a feature we had to learn to live with. For bathing we were fortunate, since only half a mile away there was a bathing place in the *falaj* for al-Ain village.

We had been in the fort only a short time when we were visited by the bailiff of the Shaikh of Buraimi village itself on the Sultan's side of the oasis. His name was Sayyid Kamil and he worked for Shaikh Saqr bin Sultan al-Naimi, the Paramount of the Naim and Al Bu Shams tribes, that is to say, the leading shaikh on the Muscat side. The administration of the district from Buraimi to Dhank in the south was in Saqr's hands, and in Dhank he had a governor. He was supposed also to be in control of the area to the north belonging to Shaikh Ubaid bin Juma of the Bani Kaab, but that shaikh was not always so willing to admit Saqr's paramountcy. His tribe was quite separate from the Naim, but the Sultan had decreed that Saqr was to be chief of all the shaikhs. Saqr, we were told, was unpopular locally and had a reputation for toughness; he was, however, the Sultan's man and it was through him that we must deal with the bedouin on the Sultan's side of the frontier.

The villages of the oasis area are typical of much of the interior of Oman. They lie at the northern end of the extensive Dhahirah plain. This plain is at about 1,000 feet above sea level and is blocked on the whole of its north-eastern edge by the range of the Oman mountains. Running through this range to the sea, there are three or four main valleys which give access to the Batinah coast, but at that time only on foot or by animal transport; they had not yet been opened up to motor traffic. To the west towards Saudi Arabia stretched the sand, and not a single permanent building stood between us and Hufuf in Saudi Arabia, some 300 miles away.

The village houses were made of mud-brick walls about ten feet high with flat roofs supported on thick beams made of palm trunks. These beams had to be frequently repaired or replaced as they had little strength and became the home of insects, especially hornets. One house I lived in was noted for the arrival each evening of thousands of these insects which would stay quietly in their holes in the beams until dawn when, after a preliminary circuit round the room, they would fly off again; alarming at first, but one got used to it and I was never stung. They all returned together at sunset and flew straight back to their nest in the ceiling.

A particular characteristic of these villages was their forts. Each village had several, varying from single watch towers, usually round, and about thirty feet in height, with a crenellated top, to those in which the shaikhs lived, large buildings with a maze of one-storeyed rooms surrounded by curtain walls, with turrets at the corners and over the gate. Others again were taller three-storey blocks or towers with several rooms on each floor. All were of the same sun-dried brick, and for each fort which was still in use and in good condition, there would be many which had long since become ruins; and these ruined turrets graced the edges of every village. Buraimi itself had a large fort with a round tower at each of its four corners guarding the entrance of the village.

I was now to see on the ground what I had heard of in Bahrain, that although our concession was signed with the Sultan, and our payments all went to him, and although the Sultan was happy for us to prospect in certain areas of the interior, and in this one in particular, the tribes also wanted a direct payment from the Company to them. Despite the fact that they looked to the Sultan as their only overlord, there was no central administration which reached out effectively to their area, and they felt that the actual land was really theirs, even though it had to be admitted that the Sultan was their Ruler.

To understand their position, it is necessary to put aside all Western ideas of sovereignty. The bedouin take from a situation very much what the maintenance of their tribal rights requires, and their needs may differ markedly in character from place to place in Arabia as we have seen. In Duru country and among the Al Bu Shams and some other bedouin tribes of the south and west of Oman, there is complete exclusivity of ownership of tribal grazing grounds. The Duru area is so large, so inhospitable and difficult to enter that before the day of the car (before 1954 in their region) they were impregnable in their fastness. No other tribe would dare enter their area for any reason, and whenever clashes took place with trespassers across their borders, fighting would be inevitable, leading to feuds with other tribes. The probable reason for excluding others almost totally was the presence of salt and sulphur deposits in their area, deposits which they worked and would allow no one else to approach.

Coming nearer to the hills and the sown land where settled people lived, this exclusivity was modified. Travellers who were acceptable could cross such semi-settled areas, and rights lay in ownership of ground for tilling or chopping of trees and especially the use of water for crops. Even here a traveller would be wise to take precautions, and the best safeguard, of which I made frequent use in later journeys, was to travel with a companion from some other tribe that was not at war with the tribe which inhabited the area one wished to cross.

In about the year 1800, the Saudis had captured Buraimi, the Muscat part of the oasis, and made their presence felt over much of the interior of Oman without directly ruling it in the modern sense. Their occupation of Buraimi was only intermittent, covering thirteen seperate periods in between which they had retreated; and in 1869 they were driven out finally by the then Imam of Oman. In the mid twenties of this century Saudi tax collectors came into the area on two or three occasions. This may have been a half-hearted attempt at a return to their previous position, but it was ineffective.

Such was the fame of King Abdul Aziz Ibn Saud that when Bertram Thomas (then one of the Sultan's ministers) came into the region in the 1920s, he was told that the people of Buraimi at that moment accepted Ibn Saud as king. People in an area not directly administered tended to be fickle about their allegiance and would, if one powerful personality were increasing in strength, attach themselves to him but, as it were, with fingers crossed. I am sure, however, that they did not accept the king as their ruler in the 1920s. It was simply a ruse to keep the foreigner, Thomas, out and as such it plainly worked. Later the Saudis quoted this as proof of their sovereignty, but I thought that this point was not a valid one to support their claim.

At the time I came to live in al-Ain, in 1948 and early 1949, there was no talk of the Saudis. The only powers recognized in Oman were that of the Sultan and the triumvirate of shaikhs in central Oman, consisting of the Ibadhi Imam and the leaders of the two factions, the Hinawiya and the Ghafiriya, but the Imam and his two shaikhly colleagues had no authority whatever in Buraimi or in the Dhahirah as a whole, and it is not even Ibadhi country, unlike most of Oman. There was one merchant living in al-Buraimi village, who claimed to be a Saudi and he was always referred to as 'the Najdi'. As to the villages on the al-Ain side of the oasis they had belonged to the Abu Dhabi shaikhs for a very long time and never to the Saudis.

The area between Abu Dhabi and Saudi Arabia was frequented by both Abu Dhabi and Saudi bedouin in search of pasture, and for this purpose was used by groups of tribes migrating, sometimes because of a bad drought in any one area which drove them to seek water and grazing elsewhere. It was also very occasionally used by pilgrims on their way to Mecca, but these would be local bedouin tribesmen, as all other pilgrims would go by sea to the Saudi ports. I could find no evidence for a normal caravan trade route between Saudi Arabia and Oman. This desert crossing was so difficult that travellers preferred to go by sea. Only the real bedouin of the high sands would attempt it.

The position in the difficult Omani area south of Buraimi, we hoped, was that the tribes would now accept Shaikh Saqr as their paramount and would, on his ordering it, allow us in. We were assured that the Sultan had recently reaffirmed all this in writing to Shaikh Saqr as the paramount shaikh of the tribes of the Naim, Al Bu Shams and Bani Kaab; and he had directed him to deal with the Company and arrange with the other shaikhs so that our geological work could begin.

Our intention was first to ensure that this plan was in good order and then go down to Muscat by truck with a small party of our Company geologists and motor up to Buraimi, making a new, hitherto unused, route for vehicles up the Wadi (valley) al-Jizzi from the Omani coast at Suhar, which we hoped the Sultan had cleared sufficiently. I realized that Dick Bird was far from confident that the Sultan's authority would suffice, but the Company was determined to observe correctly the terms of the concession, and this meant we would deal only with him. If, on the contrary, we were to give any sizeable sum to the tribes, they would treat this as a new concession, and in the event of oil being found could say that it was theirs, and that they were independent of the Sultan for this purpose. We, therefore, had to play the game the Sultan's way.

The tribes of the Dhahirah and the Duru, in particular to the south of it, had at that time very little source of revenue. Their shaikhs needed money to administer their tribes. The Sultan had a regular revenue, but it was small and he had found the state finances in deficit when he took over seventeen years earlier, and he was determined not to allow this to happen again. Therefore, apart from minor presents to shaikhs when they visited Muscat, he felt he could not afford to give significant sums to his tribal leaders, and he insisted that they must obey his orders to permit oil prospecting without any financial help. I found it difficult to believe that we would succeed if we worked on these lines, and, unless the Sultan could either show his strength in some way or pay money, I thought he would not be able to persuade the shaikhs to accept the Company in their area. However, we had no alternative but to follow the policy our London office had laid down.

We felt free to call on Shaikh Zayed to advise us, and his friendly influence over the tribes immediately to the south of Buraimi was considerable; his support of the Sultan's position in the area through the Abu Dhabi shaikhs had historical precedent in that his grandfather and other forebears all worked closely with the Sultan of Muscat. Shaikh Zayed was always constructive in his relations with the Omanis and worked for the common good. It seems quite clear to me that he wanted us to find oil in Abu Dhabi where we were already working, but he was glad to see Oman prosper as well.

Although Shaikh Saqr lived only a mile and a half away in Buraimi fort, it took us some time to arrange to see him. When Sayyid Kamil called on us we asked him to arrange an interview, but Saqr was by no means easily committed. We were also still awaiting the return of Shaikh Zayed from his hunting trip.

We busied ourselves with checking our store of petrol, of which about a third had been lost by leakage while being carried by the camels, tidying up the fort at Jahili, mending a dangerous-looking beam in the roof and doing a little exploring around the oasis. Dick seemed to know everyone, and after a break of seven or eight months was carrying on the bedouin gossip where he had dropped it at the end of the last season. He had a disarming and pleasant way, and after greeting the head of the house, would fold up his long legs to settle down and chat with an easy familiarity, remembering the interests and recent history of the person to whom he was talking, for this is exactly what the bedouin expected. They had excellent memories, and they expected you to remember all you had heard about them. They, likewise, have disconcertingly exact memories of all you have said in the past.

The villages were beautiful in early winter; the climate dry and warm by day and cool by night. Sometimes we would be invited to sit in a snug little room on the first floor of a brick house overlooking a garden. In the garden were date palms and, between the trees, alfalfa (lucerne). The rows of trees were intersected by irrigation channels, whose mud sluices would be broken and built up again systematically on a time-table to let the water run through by rotation every day or two in each part of the gardens. The water came from underground channels by gravity from underground springs that were, in some instances, as much as seven miles away under the foot of Jebel Hafit. There was a superintendent for each *falaj*, called the *Arif*. He kept in a book a record of water rights and the payment (*naub*) for them.

In the mornings the gardens would be very still, the only sounds a few birds, some parakeets and the creaking of the rope at a well worked by oxen. There were then no mechanical pumps and the noise of a car was a rarity. Among the palms, the gardens were a lush green with the darker green of Indian almond and other trees, and here and there the gash of

His Highness Shaikh Zayed bin Sultan al-Nahyan   (*R.Codrai*)

Pearl merchants and their wares (*R.Codrai*)

A pearling boat sets out for the season (*R.Codrai*)

Camels crossing the ford to Abu Dhabi before the causeway had been built
c. 1949 (*R.Codrai*)

A desert expedition. The author is standing in the truck (*R.Codrai*)

Sabir bin Muhammad (*P.D.T.C.*)

We had no four-wheel drive in 1949
(*R.Codrai*)

Water taxi, Dubai 1949   (*R.Codrai*)

When one breaks down we all stop   (*R.Codrai*)

'Spudding in' at Ras Sadr, February 1950. In the centre is Shaikh Shakhbut; on his left, Patrick Stobart, British Political Officer, and the author; Ronald Codrai is on the other side   (*R.Codrai*)

His Highness Shaikh Shakhbut, Ruler of Abu Dhabi   (*R.Codrai*)

Building of the causeway to Abu Dhabi, 1950   (*R.Codrai*)

Company vehicles on the borders of Oman   (*R.Codrai*)

His Highness Shaikh Rashid bin Humaid at the Company house in Dubai in 1949.
Among those with him, left to right, are Shaikh Ali bin Rashid, Ron Codrai, the
shaikh's secretary, the author and Muhammad Abdul Rahman who was on the staff
of the Company   (*R.Codrai*)

Husain Khan Sahib   (*R.Codrai*)

colour of bougainvillea splashing down from a wall or a tree. Sometimes we would be invited to sit and talk in the gardens in an arbour, an outdoor *majlis*, or sitting place. Then, a large woven straw mat would be put in front of us and covered with bowls of dates, nuts, figs, pomegranates and pawpaws, while coffee and tea were served, the coffee in the tiny cups without handles and the tea in small glasses.

Conversation rose and fell; neighbours dropped in for a talk. The oasis seemed so remote from modern life and so full of contentment. The fact that no one had much money really did not seem to worry people, and I envied them a way of life I could only share for a short time.

On one such visit we called on Shaikh Muhammad bin Khalifah, the senior member by descent of the Abu Dhabi ruling family. Here was a patriarch, interested in his people, his gardens, in hawking and visiting the countryside. He had gardens also near Suhar on the Batinah coast, and he was knowledgeable about animals, the digging of wells and water channels. Dressed like any of his followers in a white headcloth, black head-rope, white *thaub*, a thin *abba* (cloak) hanging from his shoulders with a gold embroidered edging, he wore at his belt a curved silver-handled dagger and on his feet the roughest locally made leather sandals. He talked in a soft voice, screwing up his eyes in the sunlight, always ready to see a joke in the passing scene. His people caught his mood and joined in. There was always laughter in his circle. Zayed, he said, would be with us tomorrow, or the next day perhaps.

Two days later we called on Shaikh Zayed at Al-Muwaiqi fort. This was rather a forbidding square fortress with crenellated corner towers. To exclude the heat, the rooms inside were necessarily rather dark and had no furniture but the colourful rugs and cushions on the floor. Shaikh Zayed was then perhaps thirty years old. He was handsome with humorous and intelligent eyes, of fine presence and bearing, simply dressed, like his cousin Muhammad, and clearly a man of action and resolution. Although he was young and had only been formally in charge of the Abu Dhabi sector of the oasis and its surrounding deserts for some two years, he was experienced in the politics of the region and was already by far the most prominent personality in the area. He had a sure touch with the bedouin in both the Abu Dhabi and Muscat areas. His brother Shaikh Shakhbut, the Ruler, lived mostly in Abu Dhabi but would reside sometimes at his fort at al-Muwaiqi. The Ruler had a considerable reputation and was a man who commanded great respect.

Both Shaikh Zayed and his brother, the Ruler (whom I was to visit later in Abu Dhabi), showed a warmth of friendship and co-operation towards us, and we had many pleasant evenings in Shaikh Zayed's *majlis* while we were in the oasis. Shaikh Zayed said that Saqr was being difficult over a number of matters, but this was only Saqr's habit. He listened to our plans for bringing up the geologists from Muscat and, although he thought it might not work, at least he considered it worth trying. He expected some opposition to our plans from the Bani Kaab and from Muhammad Salimin bin Rahmah, shaikh of the bedouin section of the Al Bu Shams tribe. After a while we made our farewells, saying that we must now call on Saqr who had agreed to see us. 'I hope the old fox gives you coffee,' said one of our friends as we parted.

6

The Search Continues

The 'old fox' did give us coffee, but it was very cold coffee, and 'cold coffee' was the common term used to describe him. We motored over the light-coloured sand in front of al-Buraimi fort and up to its gloomy portal. Sabir had to knock many times before a small shutter opened and part of a face showed itself which proved to be that of Saqr himself. With some noise and evident difficulty, he eventually unbarred the door and let us in. He seemed to be attended by only one servant, and he was reputed to spend the night with only one trusted retainer in the fortress. He was renowned for the money he held in the fort and seemed perpetually afraid equally of burglary from without and treason from within. Even Dick's easy way with the bedouin made no impression here. He was a small man, rather stout; he sat and waited for us to talk after he had, with apparent reluctance, shown us into a tiny and very dark room close to the fort's entrance, with a plain rush mat on the floor and nothing else to grace it.

Despite this introduction, the conversation went surprisingly well. The shaikh had heard from the Sultan that the geologists might come, and if his fellow shaikhs were agreeable, he said they might start working in the area between Buraimi and Dhank. He added that they must not go into Dhank itself, but he wanted some 'help'. This was the difficulty. Saqr really wanted his own oil concession and a large amount of money. He also wanted work to start, and he did not like to upset the Sultan. We realized he was struggling to choose between those conflicting aims.

It was agreed that the shaikh of the Kaab tribe and two shaikhs of the Al Bu Shams, Rashid of Hamasah and Muhammad Salimin bin Rahmah, would meet us at Saqr's fort in three days' time to agree finally to the arrival of the geologists. We did not meet in three days, nor in four, nor five. We asked various friends to help and they did their best. We made approaches through Sayyid Kamil, to no effect; we saw Saqr twice more, and on one visit we did not even get cold coffee. We were given a variety of different stories as to why the meeting did not take place, but we were assured that the shaikhs concerned were not now very far off and we were to provide the transport to bring them from an appointed meeting place in the desert. We agreed to do so but arrangements fell through. At last, after two weeks of this, we heard that they had arrived and Sayyid Kamil came over to say that our cars were to go out to fetch them and they would come at 11 a.m. Western-style time. At the time in Oman they still used the Arabic clock by which the day starts at sunset as if it were 0.00 hrs and is adjusted daily.

When we reached Saqr's fort the scene was quite different from the previous occasion. There was a large number of camels and other animals outside. Our own two pick-ups which had brought the shaikhs were there with Firdullah and Sabir, the latter grinning happily. There was a group of bedouin on either side of the door squatting in the shade of the fortress wall and, wonder of wonders, the door itself was half open but held by a chain.

Sabir ducked into the fort under the chain to announce our arrival to the shaikhs, but it was some time before the chain was unhooked and the door opened. Saqr was never one to show any form of enthusiasm at the arrival of a visitor. After greeting us in his usual sulky style, he took us to a rather larger room already crammed full of people. Here were all the other shaikhs and their followers. They stood and we shook hands with each and, finally, a tiny space was made for us to sit on the floor next to Saqr. Then an endless and futile discussion began right away about the money we were to pay. Dick did his best to ride this out, emphasizing that Saqr was their declared spokesman, that he had agreed, and that the Sultan had agreed, to our operating without any specific payment to them. He explained we would pay for labour and services rendered, but no concession payment as such was permitted. The meeting went on until two o'clock, and, uniquely for Arabia, without coffee or any other refreshment; it finally broke up inconclusively by our leaving it.

The shaikhs stayed in the area but not as the guests of Saqr. We called on them separately and they called on us. It all came down to money and they each wanted more than could be passed off as a modest *douceur*. In the course of the next ten days, small unofficial *douceurs* did change hands and sufficient agreement with the shaikhs seemed to be reached to

make a visit by the geologists worth while. Dick and I went back to Dubai
to link up with the geologists who were to come to Muscat with us and
then return to Buraimi by the Batinah and the Wadi al-Jizzi. We left two
of our people to look after our things at Jahili. At Dubai we picked up
three more vehicles which had been shipped in for this expedition and
were joined by three geologists and a surveyor. We made our way over
the desert and then down the coast to Muscat to pay our respects to the
Sultan before beginning our journey back to Buraimi.

The journey in those days was of considerable interest as there were
then very few vehicles which made this trip. There were no roads, and
across the first forty miles of low sand dunes the going was rough and
bumpy. In that particular year, there had been a number of incidents in
which the bedouin from the far south had shot up and robbed both car
and camel convoys; for this reason traffic was particularly slack, and we
met no other vehicle until well inside Muscat territory. According to
some unwritten code the bedouin were not supposed to attack us as
guests and foreigners but fortunately on this occasion we did not even
encounter any hostile bedouin. We had no guards with us.

After crossing the sand dunes, the track became better defined and led
up a long *wadi* into the mountains. The mountain range of Oman is
mostly of bare wind-polished rock, beautiful at a distance but harsh and
forbidding from close to. A very rough track, strewn with boulders, led
us through a rocky pass at about one thousand feet and on down the other
side until, turning a corner in the narrow *wadi*, we glimpsed the sea.
There the track flattened out on to a narrow plain with the mountains on
the right and on the left rows of palms and gardens; beyond them lay a
golden beach and the sea.

We camped that night on the Batinah coast in almost idyllic
conditions. Because there is some malaria there, we carried mosquito
nets; they also saved us from the attentions of the first morning flies. We
tied the mosquito nets to a convenient tree, unrolled our beds, and that
was our camp. The journey onwards next day was almost monotonously
attractive, but the going was rough and very bumpy as the track wound
its way among seemingly endless date gardens and tiny villages. We left
some of our party at Suhar and in two trucks went on to meet His
Highness the Sultan, in Muscat.

Muscat was then a fascinating little town. It is set in a crater which
makes a horeshoe bay with dark crags at either end of the waterfront

overlooking the sea. The circle of the waterfront was mostly taken up by the neat white palace, a government office and the British Consulate General nestling under the crag at the far end. On top of the crags were two old Portuguese forts, one used as the Treasury and the other as the prison. Both overlooked the little town which lay cupped in the rocks. The town was built of small white houses and was surrounded by an ancient wall, which in places ran right up the rocky slope behind the buildings. Only two streets within the wall were large enough to admit cars, but in those days there was virtually no motor traffic anyway. There were some curious and maddening rules and restrictions, most of which still applied until 1970: Europeans were not allowed out at night unless accompanied by an Omani carrying a lamp; special permission had to be obtained to drive a vehicle inside the wall; no smoking was allowed in the main streets; and musical instruments, including radios, were not allowed to be played anywhere in public, and only behind thick walls in private. These were some of the general restrictions, but far more onerous were those which were suffered by the Omani people themselves. The European community at that time averaged only about nine, including a Bank manager and the British Consul General, with whom we were to stay.

We found the Sultan in excellent spirits. Urbane, courteous and very well-informed, he lived in a simple yet elegant and dignified style. The palace was a well-built two-storey white building on the edge of the harbour. On entering the tall studded doors through a little postern set in one of them, there was a wide flight of highly polished stone steps at the top of which the Sultan's secretary was waiting to greet the visitor and to conduct him to the Sultan's reception room. This was simply but tastefully furnished and had wide open windows which gave on to the shimmering blue and silver of the harbour. The room was cool, and airy and the bare floor highly polished. The Sultan, who was dressed in a flowing robe and wearing an impressive and elaborate coloured turban, purple, white and red, rose to greet us. He spoke softly in almost perfect English. He was extremely courteous and dignified.

We reached general agreement on the area which the geologists were to examine in the country which lay south of Buraimi. The area which this might open to us would only be part of the Dhahirah, and although it might be of value to look at the rocks in this area, our main objective was still over a hundred miles further south. If Saqr took us into his territory, it would be no more than a step in the right direction. The Sultan said he was arranging for us to go further south and into the Duru area later. He was most insistent that we should pay no rentals to the shaikhs, and our meeting passed pleasantly, as he could be charming in an interview. He promised to attach an effective government official named Yusuf to our party to help us with the tribes. We left the Sultan with the feeling that we could not get anything more from him but that what he had agreed to might not suffice. We prayed that the official might turn out to be a man of influence and purpose.

Early on the following day, we again took the long, bumpy and suffocatingly dusty track up the coast past the hundreds of beautiful date gardens and by late evening joined the rest of the party near Suhar on the Batinah coast. Yusuf the Sultan's trusted official was there to see us up the valley of the Jizzi. He was pleasant enough, but we could see at once that he had little or no authority or presence. We did not expect him to be of much help, and help from the government was what was needed. The Sultan himself had ordered the villagers to make a track up the valley which our cars were to negotiate. We spent the night at Suhar and looked at the fine old Portuguese fort and great square tower which dominated the town. The gardens at Suhar were particularly beautiful, and the water was plentiful and sweet. Early next day, we loaded our vehicles and set off up the *wadi*. We soon left the plantations behind us and began crossing the grey rocky plain, not difficult driving but hard on our springs. As we came into the foothills, we were forced to drop down into the valley bottom; but there had been recent rain in the mountains and there were intermittent pools of water in the *wadi* bed. These we negotiated as best we could, sometimes going round them, sometimes through. We began to reach habitations, small villages perched on low bluffs near the *wadi* bed but high enough to be clear of flash floods which can suddenly sweep down these valleys without warning, carrying everything with them that lies in their path.

It was near the first village that trouble began with the vehicles. We could find no clear way round a particularly deep pool and had to use crowbars to clear a path round it through the boulders, with difficulty pushing and pulling the vehicles through the rocks on the pool's edge. When we came up to the village, we were immediately asked into one of the houses and entertained with coffee and mounds of dates served on basket mats. We asked after the track which was supposed to have been made as we could not see one. Our hosts took us across to see it. It was on the other side of the *wadi* bed, very rough indeed and not nearly wide enough; in fact virtually useless. The villagers told us, I am sure in all innocence, that they did not expect our vehicles to be so wide. We had to make up for the inadequacies of the track by the use of crowbars to clear the bigger rocks and the work was laborious; although the difficult stretch was only a matter of a few miles, it took us from morning until nearly sunset to cover it.

As we toiled up this difficult sector, the sun became hotter, the way dustier. The valley sides which had been gentle slopes became steeper, the dried *wadi* bed varying from twenty feet in width to a hundred yards. In places it had three or four feet of water in it, but mostly it was dry. Sometimes the *wadi* bed took 'U' turns and we were able at a few of these places to climb over spurs to shorten our journey. The grey rocks were bare, polished and shining in the sun; but where the hard rock disappeared into the gravel and stones of the *wadi* bed, oleander sprouted luxuriantly. At places, looking up side valleys, we could see villages high in the rocks with a few palms or fig trees on tiny terraces hacked out of the cliff. At others, there were small plantations of palms and groups of huts right down in the valley only a few feet above what seemed to be the possible flood line, and at such places the villagers would come out and look at us in astonishment.

The tribesmen lower in the *wadi* offered us a gang of workers to help us to push the trucks through the difficult places. Yusuf, the Sultan's representative, had at last admitted he was a newcomer to the area, like ourselves, but he agreed to a dozen Shawami tribesmen joining us. They jumped on to our trucks and were to come with us as far as Hail and Rabi, two villages mid-way up the *wadi*. We continued slowly and noisily with more than one hold-up to clear rocks. The front truck was just negotiating a particularly deep stretch of water, which we could see no way of avoiding, when we were greeted by a crackle of musketry, and one or two bullets came singing by us, ricocheting on the rocks around us. Needless to say, we all stopped and the front truck stuck right in the water. Both Sabir and Firdullah characteristically laughed at this apparent misfortune. We switched off our engines and in the sudden silence after their roaring, the atmosphere seemed tense, brittle and electric. A few more shots came from a low bluff about a hundred yards to our front and fifty yards above us. There were shouts from above and we shouted back explaining we were friends and had the Sultan's blessing. Then Yusuf took up the story and joined us in the shouting game.

We had all climbed off the trucks which straggled down a steep and difficult boulder-strewn slope to the leading truck which looked half submerged now in the water. The slope was exposed to the tribesmen who were firing at us, and they were in good positions on the bluff above the water in front of us. They had us at their mercy; there was no getting back and no cover within two hundred yards of us, or more, in any direction. Yusuf had a rifle and, I remembered with some concern, so did one or two of the excitable Shawamis; but they were by this time crouching behind the tail boards of the vehicles on which they had been riding, and those in the front truck had perforce to crouch in the water. Inevitable at such moments thoughts of other such incidents in Oman's history came to mind in which the victims either did or did not live to walk away.

Eventually two men appeared on the bluff and invited Yusuf to come forward. Yusuf did go forward a little, and we could hear the echoes of a shouted talk. He came back to us some minutes later and said that the villagers knew all about us and that as the Sultan had warned them of the trip, they would let us through with pleasure. But, why had we picked up those beastly Shawamis? Everyone knew, but not us and certainly not Yusuf, that Shawamis were not allowed on the territory of these two villages, and their plan to come as part of our party was just a trick to get them over forbidden ground. If we left them behind and took on some of their own villagers instead as helpers, we could go through.

In due course, but not without the Shawamis making a great noise, agreement was reached. We walked up to the village which was only just past the bluff, and we were offered coffee and dates: honour was satisfied. The disgruntled Shawamis went home on foot, having been paid off liberally to compensate them, and we took on a like number of the Bani Ghaith tribe who assured us that they were acceptable all the way up to Buraimi. So, it turned out, was the case. Our worst physical troubles with the 'going' coincided with the political hold-up, but the Bani Ghaith showed us a way round the wide water obstacle, and with their help we cleared a passable track. Soon after leaving the village, we saw that we were now near the watershed and had come out of the area of habitation. From here onwards the valley was nearly barren, the rocks brown and grey. They rose on both sides steeply to the serrated mountain tops, the *wadi* bed itself being only twenty yards wide; and we mostly found our way along tracks made by animals some twenty feet up at the side of the gorge, not without some excitement and alarm as we put our trucks through places which their makers could not have had in mind for them. If only we had four-wheel-drive vehicles! Land Rovers and jeeps had yet to become available.

From the watershed, about 1200 feet above sea level, the going became gradually easier and nearly level until we came out at sunset between two arms of black crags on to the Dhahirah plain, and there in front of us was the familiar whale-back of Jebel Hafit. Turning northwards, we were soon among the trees and found our way across the bumpy gravel towards Buraimi. It was dark and rather cold when we got into the village. We dropped Yusuf there, at his request, and paid off the Bani Ghaith. It was not until 10 p.m. that we got back to fort Jahili. We had been at it since five in the morning, and were tired but happy to have got through. A brew of tea, our bedrolls laid down on the sand, and that was enough for the day.

Yusuf had fresh instructions from the Sultan to give to Shaikh Saqr, and we had a succession of meetings with tribal leaders on the following days. The geologists did manage a few trips a little into the Dhahirah, but Ibri and the south remained places we could not reach, and for that reason they began to have a strange fascination for me. What were they like, these places we could not visit? Clearly, we were still making no progress and the geologists, although they could find a little work to do on the Abu Dhabi side, were wasting their time. Both Yusuf and Saqr thought that it might help with the other tribes if Sayyid Ahmad bin Ibrahim, Minister of the Interior in Muscat, could come up and talk to them. We could hardly refuse to support this idea, and I set off with Sabir and two pick-ups, on our own, all the way down the Jizzi again to see if I could persuade him to come from the capital.

Remembering the toil and trouble coming up, I expected that we would have trouble going down again, but Sabir assured me that if we took two empty trucks and two or three spare hands to help push us, we should be all right. Apart from an alarming moment when the truck I was driving stuck near Hail, with one wheel on the edge of a fifty-foot drop, all was well. We spent about an hour digging out rocks to widen the track at that point and we found that the rest of the track, though still rather difficult, was now usable. We had started early and reached Suhar in the early afternoon and began the trip down the coast to Muscat on the same day. The tribesmen on the trip down were all very friendly, but then we were careful to avoid any mixture of Shawamis and Bani Ghaith. Together they were a riot, but separately all smiles, coffee and dates.

The following day we reached Muscat and the Sultan agreed to Sayyid Ahmad's trip to Buraimi. Sayyid Ahmad was, even in those days, a venerable figure with a flowing white beard and, like the Sultan, he wore an elaborate turban. Charming and cheerful, he was an excellent companion. We travelled together in his aged Ford as far as Suhar, where I was lodged in a little villa belonging to the Sultan, in a lovely garden a mile or so to the north-west of the town, while Sayyid Ahmad stayed in the town at the Customs Post.

Early next morning, he sent me up by truck from Suhar an excellent but, needless to say, rather cold breakfast of boiled milk, bread, dates and a kind of porridge; and he followed shortly afterwards. We set off in my two vehicles as Sayyid Ahmad's was not strong enough to face the Jizzi, with myself driving in the lead and Sabir bringing up the rear. Sayyid Ahmad had insisted on bringing several followers and quite a lot of gear so that we were overloaded, but I readily agreed, provided only that the followers walked over the very bad patches and pushed when necessary. I knew it would be hopeless to attempt to refuse this unwanted escort, since no man of importance can travel without followers in Oman if he is to retain the respect of the people.

With some misgivings we set off over the rough plain. Neither Sayyid Ahmad nor I were anxious to stop at each village; he because it meant giving a largesse; I because of the time it would need. The people were all glad to see him and wanted to give us lunch everywhere, but Sayyid Ahmad managed to prevent sheep being killed in his honour, and we got to Hail soon after noon. There we had trouble with the vehicles. The steep pitches could not be negotiated with all the followers on the back, and the followers did not want to get off. However, after a particularly hair-raising slide, with wheels spinning, towards a nasty little drop to the *wadi* bed below, Sayyid Ahmad was thoroughly convinced that I was right, and at a snapped order from him all the men got down with alacrity and began to push. My trouble then was to persuade Sayyid Ahmad that it was all right for them to get on again. 'No,' he said. 'They have legs, let them walk.' However, we reached a compromise which allowed them to get on the running board of my pick-up, hanging to the sides, ready to jump down, and we made much better progress. Nevertheless, it was dark when we got into Buraimi and eventually said goodbye to Sayyid Ahmad at Saqr's fort. Next morning Sayyid Ahmad seemed to be doing rather better with Saqr that we had, but such was the kaleidoscope of tribal politics that Saqr in turn was getting on worse with Obaid of the Bani Kaab, and with both Rashid and bin Rahmah of the settled and nomadic Al Bu Shams.

To appreciate the intricacies of this situation, one has to remember that each shaikh is living publicly in front of his people, and if he appears to be weakening he will lose the authority he has over them and, with it, his position altogether. A shaikh obviously has to be acceptable to remain in power. He has been elected by his tribe and, if he appears to be failing to lead and benefit his people, they will begin to desert him. Only a very assured shaikh, who has built up a strong position over a period, can make decisions which concern the future of the tribe as a whole without going through at least the appearance of some process of consultation. Shaikh Zayed, alone of the shaikhs in the Dhahirah, was in a really strong position, but he was not directly involved as far as our entry to the south was concerned, except as a friend and adviser to both parties.

Of the Sultanate shaikhs, Saqr was in the most peculiar position. Over-careful with money, he kept the proceeds of local taxes in his fort in boxes full of silver. He had a strong but small group of armed men both in Buraimi and in Dhank, forty miles to the south. He owned and farmed more irrigated land than any other Sultanate shaikh in this area; he was feared for his toughness, but he had no popular following outside his immediate retainers. He maintained his position only with difficulty and, uniquely in this area, on the basis of his wealth and his group of armed retainers, rather than on popular acceptance.

Shaikh Obaid of the Kaab had a good presence and clearly had leadership; a pleasing personality, he was popular with his tribesmen. Rashid of the settled Al Bu Shams had a reputation for being over-careful with money and was not popular; he resented the paramountcy of Saqr over the Naim and Al Bu Shams tribes (the two tribes were structurally one). Bin Rahmah was shaikh of the Al Bu Shams bedouin group; he was clever and seemed to have considerable leadership.

From the secondhand accounts we received through Yusuf of the negotiations, it seemed Sayyid Ahmad was getting nowhere with anyone but Saqr who appeared to be becoming more and more isolated from the other leaders. Perhaps to try to show us that he wished to co-operate, Saqr suggested that the geologists should begin work on a small hill to the south of Buraimi. Early one morning we set off as arranged, calling at the fort for Saqr who wanted to watch the geologists at work. As might be expected, he kept us waiting an inordinate time to show how important he was, and when he came to the door of the fort he hardly deigned to reply to my greeting. I showed him into the front of Dick's pick-up and off we went in silence. Even when we got to the rocks, Saqr would hardly say a word. He and Dick and I sat by idly, alternately drinking coffee and tea, while the geologists pottered about and collected some samples which they put into small bags and labelled. After a couple of hours, Dick suggested we should pack up for the day. It was really only a trial morning and the shaikh was, not surprisingly, looking very bored by such a dull occasion. As the geologists packed up their gear, the sample bags were collected and put into one truck.

Immediately the shaikh noticed and said, 'What are you doing with those?' Dick explained that they would be sorted out, examined and cut into fine pieces for microscopic examination, the most interesting ones being sent to London for further tests. The shaikh said that he thought that if they were worth sending to London, they must be worth a lot of money. He would keep these samples, and as for the future an 'arrangement' would have to be made.

For someone with no knowledge of the outside world and only recently introduced to such things as car and radio, the technique of oil production was something he could not possibly be expected to know, and his request in these circumstances was not unreasonable, but it was a warning, if such were needed, of what lay ahead.

The next three days were taken up with talks between Sayyid Ahmad and the shaikh. But he had to report that he had reached no really satisfactory conclusion and, as the best season climatically for geological work would come to an end within a month, we decided to delay our project until the following year, and we recommended in this sense to our London office. I drove Sayyid Ahmad back to Suhar and had a much easier trip. On our journey up, he had given instructions for parts of the track to be improved and this had been done. Also we now knew its difficult points and we managed to get him to Suhar and ourselves back in Jahili all in one day.

By now the track looked almost as well established as the other routes which we had been using, and it demonstrated that in Oman the passage of a few trucks is enough to establish a well-worn main route at once.

We spent the rest of the spring between Jahili and Dubai. The last weeks were hot and trying, and in the early afternoon we used to sit in the comparatively cool irrigation channels to make the afternoon heat endurable. I remember that period of spring in Buraimi and al-Ain for the pleasant visits to see Shaikh Zayed, and others. These were evening meals sitting on a rug in the sands, or lunch in a date garden beside the clear water of the irrigation channels, all in the atmosphere of quiet and remoteness which the oasis still had in those days.

Although I was still a newcomer to Oman, I already felt rather despondent about the future – would we be permitted to search for the oil in Oman? Here was a people friendly, lively, delightful; yet, what future had they otherwise? The chances of oil in the area south of Buraimi were, we hoped, very good indeed. The Sultan did not have enough money to administer the area from his far-away capital. The history of the bedouin tribes in Jordan, Iraq and Saudi Arabia proved again and again that the bedouin will continue their raiding and tribal feuds until central authority can make itself established in the towns and, by using modern methods of communication, can reach out from the towns into the desert. Until the invention of the motor car, the modern rifle and machine gun, bedouin were undisputed masters in their deserts. Settled people can hire bedouin to fight each other, can raise guards from among them or pay them to let trade cross their land; but before the car was available to them the settled tribes found it difficult, if not impossible, to control the bedouin who could raid any line of communication which crossed their deserts or was within easy reach of them. There was one exception to this: that of any tribe which depended entirely on one particular group of settled people on the edge of the desert and thus became economically dependent on them. Such a tribe could be controlled to some degree by those in authority in the settled area. The Duru were in this special position since their roaming ground had the Empty Quarter on one side and an area of the main strength of the Imam on the other. There, in the villages, they sold their firewood, their salt and their sulphur which they carried to the villages or their borders. They received no help from Muscat and their allegiance to the Imam was by no means clear.

I felt that what was needed was for the Muscat government to do some development in the interior to show the benefits of modern government, and thus persuade the tribes to permit the central government to supervise the search for oil. The difficulty was that the government did not have the money to do this until oil was found. The key lay with the Duru tribe who alone occupied the area of prime interest. The problem was to get to them, and find and produce the oil, thus gaining enough money for the government to do the development which was so desperately needed. Otherwise it seemed the tribes would never allow exploration to take place in the desert, and the hills in Oman were of little interest to us from the point of view of oil. Therefore, as things looked, progress and development could never come to them as long as the bedouin themselves prevented the essential preparatory stages, stopping, albeit unwittingly, the search for the oil Oman so badly needed.

The difficulty in penetrating the then largely unknown Oman is well described by Wilfred Thesiger in *Arabian Sands*, 'more difficult to penetrate in 1948 than it had been when Wellstead went there more than a hundred years before'. Wilfred Thesiger of course got into its deserts but not even he could get to the heartland of the settled areas. It is amusing to recall that after a stay of several months in 1948 and 1949 in Oman, the Sultan asked the British authorities in the Gulf to cancel his Omani visa. Wilfred replied to this request with a smile, 'I never had one.'

In Abu Dhabi and the rest of the Trucial Coast there was no difficulty of access for the Company. Exploration was held up by World War II, and for a time after it, because of lack of equipment and other shortages, but from 1947 both gravity and seismic survey was fully in operation over the whole region of the Trucial Coast Emirates, and the Company was just about to drill in Abu Dhabi territory at Ras al-Sadr. The shaikhs on the Trucial Coast told us that in their view the operations were going too slowly, and I found it impossible not to sympathize with this view. But the Company maintained that it was proceeding as fast as it was able, and this was the line I had to take.

In June we finally packed up in Jahili, said goodbye to Shaikh Zayed and our other friends and returned to Dubai where I was to take over from Jacko, for the time being at least, but I was to keep in touch with Oman and be ready for further expeditions inland while Dick went home to London. From this time, my hopes centred on the Duru country and the sphinx it harboured, the anticline called Jebel Fahud, which might be full of oil.

Meanwhile, unknown to me at the time, the Saudis at the end of April 1949 laid a claim to Buraimi, including two-thirds of Abu Dhabi territory, and an undefined area of the hinterland of Oman, the claim line ending at a point in the middle of nowhere, north-east of Buraimi, indicating a vague claim to anything beyond that point. This I would learn of later, and of the consequences to our operations in the longer run.

7

A Pause between Expeditions

After the attempt which we made in 1949 to get into Oman from the north, I returned to Dubai as the Company's representative and much of my work in the following three years concerned the Trucial States. I still had some responsibility for Oman, and helped in the planning for the future. This meant some travelling to Muscat over this period. To assist in this I was to have help from a colleague in Dubai, Ronald Codrai, an Arabic speaker until recently in the Royal Air Force. Before long an electricity generator arrived which gave us light and fans and enabled us to have a refrigerator. Later still, some airconditioning sets were sent. But they were not very effective, especially as we still had no glass for windows and had to make do with a kind of perspex sheet through which you could not see.

What I remember chiefly is the very friendly reception we received everywhere in our travels in the shaikhdoms and trips to Oman and to Muscat itself. The latter I made sometimes by land sometimes by sea or in a Company aircraft, usually the little biplane De Havilland Rapide. The voyages to Muscat and to Abu Dhabi in small, locally made boats were among the most pleasant I have ever made. Journeys to Muscat by sea I made usually in the autumn, as it is the calmest season at sea in the Gulf. This was important to anyone who wanted to avoid too much excitement, since from Musendam to Muscat there is a distance of 240 miles, and on that voyage there was in those days only one safe anchorage for small boats and, in the spring and summer, storms blow up very suddenly. I used one of three boats on these expeditions: the tiny *Qanas* of Khan Sahib Hussein, which the owner said was the first powered sailing boat in the Gulf, and was only about thirty feet long; the *Shaheen*, which we hired from the Iron Oxide Company which mined iron oxide on Bu Musa island, and which was perhaps forty feet long;

and the *Fatha al-Khair*, which was about the same size.

On my first trip to Muscat, I was accompanying Dick Bird who had made the voyage before and was fond of fishing and knew the best places for fish. The second trip I made on my own. I got on board the *Fatha al Khair* in Dubai Creek and we set out in the evening on the high tide. Like all other dhows that I came across, the *Fatha al-Khair* had no accommodation built in her. Forward and amidships, there were good holds for cargo, and the aft part was devoted below decks to the small Kelvin diesel engine. The small poop deck was slightly raised above it and had beams overhead for a canvas awning. I lived on the poop deck with the captain and the helmsman, while the other members of the crew were mainly on the forward deck. The decks were flat, not cambered, and made of high-quality teak worn smooth by use, as indeed was the whole boat. The *Fatha al-Khair* was a *jalboot* class of craft.

The single mast was raked forward to allow the spar of the lateen rig to pass in front of it as the ship goes about. The main spar can be much longer than the ship, and the huge sail is not quite triangular, as are the lateen sails of the Levant, but has a fourth side on its leading lower end. The purpose of this seemed to me that it allowed the sail, when fastened to iron rings in the deck, to be held much closer to a fore and aft position than is normally possible with the lateen rig and still offer a firm leading edge to the wind. I am a layman on these matters, but I could see the contrast in the way they handled the sail when I was sailing in the Gulf of Aqaba with a plain triangular lateen rig, where it seemed to me we had much greater difficulty beating against the wind. To my eye, the Gulf sailor can turn closer to the wind and still keep the sail working. Amidships, the *Fatha al-Khair* had the usual cooking apparatus. This consists of a big wooden cowl about three feet wide and four feet high in which there is an iron grate for the charcoal fire. Passengers on the poop inevitably get a considerable share of cooking smoke, and I used to go forward whenever they were cooking if the smoke was overpowering. The other accoutrements of the ship were of the simplest. There was a large compass, purchased I was told in Kerala, and looking like a genuine antique from King's Road in London, brightly decorated in black and green. The tiller was the normal kind of wheel and was linked to the rudder by pulleys and rope. The spar, when furled and lashed, was much longer than the ship and was tied to the awning posts over our heads on the poop. The boat had a single large iron anchor with a long coir rope (I never saw one on a chain). Our boat carried a small, roughly made dinghy, and apart from cooking pots and fishing tackle, this completed our furniture.

We crossed the bar with the little Kelvin engine puffing away, its exhaust well above the waterline next to the rudder. This could be a nuisance in a following wind when the exhaust fumes might blow back on to us, but only if the wind was directly aft. Coming out of the creek, we turned up the coast and set a course parallel to it, and the whole crew pulled the ropes to set the sail while I held the tiller. The size of the crew seemed to be measured by the number of men needed to haul up the spar. Our speed in flat calm with no sail must have been about five knots, and I found they would set the mainsail whenever they could to add to the speed and also to steady the boat if the sea was at all rough. In the morning we came opposite the entrance of Khaur al-Shaam (Elphinstone's Inlet) which I had visited before with Dick Bird. At this point, the mountains of the peninsula are lower but are still several thousand feet high, and grey-brown rocks go straight down to the sea. In most places a six-foot tide has eaten away an overhang so that you could not get ashore under any of the cliffs. In places the cliffs are further back and the small rock-strewn plain is left. Wherever this happens, there will be a village such as Khasab near the entrance of the inlet.

We entered the inlet and passed by Telegraph Island, where at the beginning of the century the British had a small telegraph station for a short time. It was a terrible hardship post, and I was full of wonder at the huge rocks and the calm sea which seems to run right into the mountains. Turning a corner, the fiord opened up and extended some twelve miles to a cliff at the end. Only the chart can tell you that a mile away on the other side of the cliff is another inlet which is part of the Indian Ocean. On this occasion I gave Khasab a miss as we had not been well received there on an earlier visit and our captain said he would not put in there for anything. He said, 'Those wild Shihuh would kill us.' I am sure they would not have done, but at that time they were very suspicious of strangers and it was wise not to provoke them. They were the tribe which inhabited the peninsula and they spoke a language of their own. We sailed out of the inlet and up to the former British naval anchorage at Khaur Kawai. Here was a small island, Jazirat al Ghanam, on which you could still see parts of the buildings and wood and metal walkways along the side of the cliff to get from one building to the other. Moored in the bay there was still an old rusty floating tank which the Navy had used for fuel oil, but the place was now deserted. The brown rocks of the little island, a narrow gap of blue sea between it and the mainland and the great soaring cliffs of the peninsula made a desolate, harsh, but beautiful sight. We anchored there and caught some fish, deciding to stay the night so as to have the benefit of the first light at what we called 'Fisherman's Rock', which is a tiny islet almost at the point of the Musendam Peninsula, for at first light there was excellent fishing for king mackerel and also baracuda.

The following morning we set sail before the sun had risen and got to our islet. We spent an hour trolling with lines and caught several beautiful fish, then we set sail, south-eastwards now, towards Muscat. On this occasion we sailed through the Straits of Hormuz in daylight, but on another trip, after we had gone through the Straits at night and having passed the last rocks, the captain lashed the tiller and lay down beside it. A few hours later I woke up to find the whole crew asleep, the sail up, the engine running, no light showing, and the ship steady on her course. Far away to our port side, I could see the lights of tankers coming up to the straits. I woke the captain and said, 'No one seems to be awake.' He said, 'If you are worried, stay awake yourself,' and drowsed off again. We were, I am sure, perfectly safe, as we had plenty of open sea, and we were on a steady course. The slightest change of wind or course would have awakened the captain, and the nearest ships were a good five miles away. However, I must admit I stayed awake.

This time, sailing in daylight, having turned the point of Musendam Peninsula, we had a startling view of a fresh scene. The sea seemed to be a deeper blue and the sun, now coming from a different angle, gave everything a different aspect. The land lay on our right still but the cliffs, instead of being dark in shadow were bright in the morning sun. Sailing out of the Gulf, the land had looked gloomy until we reached the point of Musendam, but then as we sailed out into the Gulf of Oman everything seemed bright and cheerful. I had plenty of books to read, but the crew were great talkers and I would ask them about their method of navigation and other things about their calling. They produced something which looked to me like a rudimentary sextant but without any lenses which they said could be used to measure the angle between the stars and the horizon. They navigated mainly on the North Star by night and the sun by day. They had tattered old handwritten books with instructions as to the main ports and hazards on the route; however, they knew every landmark on the way. They would glance at the coast, and, if we were at all close in shore, sounding by the lead would tell them exactly where they were. They knew all the reefs and sandbanks and each one had its name. Any danger point which lay anywhere near the route they would go to look for, as 'a danger seen and passed is a danger no more'. They had complete confidence in their navigation which seemed wholly justified, based as it was on nothing less than a total knowledge of everything on their route.

We continued on down the Omani Coast keeping within sight of the shore. We looked into the village of Lima which is perched on the side of the peninsula and inaccessible from the land because of the high mountains round it: a beautiful little village of white cottages, each one perched on a rocky ledge, some above the others, which was then totally out of touch with the modern world. We went on to Dibba, which likewise in those days could not be reached by vehicle, but is now at the end of a motorway. Here again, a little village, set in a bay with palmgroves behind, but in three sections belonging respectively to Muscat, Sharjah and Fujairah. We visited the three hospitable headmen representing the three governments in Diba and took coffee and refreshments with each. Each man flew the flag of his shaikhdom, but otherwise there was no sign of any political division or enmity and the village seemed to be a single community.

To give an accurate picture of this whole area one must stress this potential division and the possibility of tribal upsets, but also the fact that normally life was peaceful. The tribal wars or feuds, as we should call them, could be fierce, but casualties were few. One of the most dramatic had been between the Shaikhs Khalid bin Sultan of Sharjah and Zayed bin Khalifah of Abu Dhabi in 1868. The former met his opponent in Sharjah, each being at the head of his army, and Shaikh Zayed shot the Shaikh of Sharjah, who fell mortally wounded in front of them all, putting an end to the fight. Shaikh Zayed went on to rule with great success for another four decades. Perhaps this gives one the rhythm of events: fighting was always possible, but peace was the norm desired. The British later tried to solve these boundary problems, but although they did much successful work they had not completed it by 1971 when their hegemony over the region ended.

We went on to Muscat where we went ashore at the British Consulate building set on the edge of Muscat Bay near the Sultan's palace. Two days later, when we were calling on His Highness, the Sultan, after greeting us, said, 'I see you came by boat.' We asked him how he knew and he said he 'happened' to be looking through his telescope and he saw us landing on the beach. Then he added rather severely, 'You didn't go through customs.' We naturally apologized for our lapse, and I will never know if he was being serious or not.

Some of my most interesting journeys were made in the company of the Khan Sahib Hussain. 'Khan Sahib' was an Indian order in the time of the Raj, similar to the orders of the British Empire such as the MBE. This came to be used as his family name, and it is still the name of the family. He was a wonderful companion, a raconteur with a superb repertoire of stories of the old days at sea in the Gulf. He always dressed beautifully in flowing robes and he wore a handsome type of turban. He had all the charm of a distinguished personality, which is what he was. His family had for many years filled the Indian Government's position of Residency Agent, stationed in Sharjah and responsible for all that government's affairs in the six Trucial States (Fujairah was not then recognized as a separate shaikhdom).

Khan Sahib was for a time assistant Residency Agent, and later Residency Agent; but much of his time had been at sea. Before World War I he had also served as a pilot on the Shatt al-Arab waterway in the Basra area. By the time I came he had become a contractor and did work for the Company. His little boat the *Qanas* was the first 'launch', that is to say a locally made craft, a *jalboot*, to be fitted with an engine, in this case a small Kelvin 75 h.p. diesel. It drew only three feet and we could take her inshore up the narrow creeks, especially those north-east of Abu Dhabi, which enabled us to avoid the rough water for at least half the journey between Dubai and Abu Dhabi if a *shamal* (the prevailing north-west wind) was blowing.

He constructed for the Company the first causeway joining Abu Dhabi island with the mainland. I had been urging our General Manager for some time to give me a little money to build a rough causeway and bridge to connect us to the capital. Without it we had to ford the quarter-mile channel at low tide, and even then cars would be in the water up to their axles. We sometimes had to remove fan belts to stop the fan throwing the water up on to the engine. If the wind blew from the north-west the tide remained high and we could not cross to Abu Dhabi.

This meant not only that I could not cross myself to call on the Shaikh, but that the Company's desert teams in the field could be cut off from Abu Dhabi. Whenever I asked the General Manager if we could do something the answer always was a testy, 'My dear fellow we are an oil company not a bridge-building company.'

One day I attended a management meeting in the London office and I thought it opportune to raise this matter. The General Manager was there and, to stop me asking, wrote me a cheque for 1,000 pounds sterling and pushed it across to me. 'You can do it with that,' he said, with a smile.

Back on the Trucial Coast I set about finding ways and means to build a causeway and bridge for almost nothing. There had to be a small bridge to let the tide through. The marine department of the Company sent a small survey ship to establish tide gauges to estimate high water, and we found that the tide went out at different times in the two creeks, which met at the point where the causeway would be. We had to let the tide through each way otherwise it would have built up on one side and pushed the causeway over. The 'camp boss' of the field party also gave me every help.

We found lying in the desert sufficient used drill pipe that was no longer of any use to the Company, and a large quantity of oil-well cement which was slightly damaged and could not be used in the exploration wells but was good enough for our purpose. They gave us a big low-loading vehicle from the Company camp and we had other trucks as we needed them. In due course a narrow, bumpy, but useable causeway was built which served everyone from 1952 until 1968, when it was replaced by a new, proper bridge, costing one million pounds sterling. Our causeway was then swept away and the channel considerably deepened to allow ships through. Only the old watchtower, which had guarded the original crossing point, remains. The new bridge is still called the *maqta* or 'crossing point'. This left the ten miles of mud-flat or *sabkhah* as an obstacle, but at least using care and a four-wheel-drive vehicle you could reach Abu Dhabi by car without having to wait for low tide.

Khan Sahib used to supply the field parties, set up their camps and do construction work for the Company. To begin with he was the only contractor who had the equipment necessary, but later others came in and jobs could be put out to tender. He usually offered the best price and we always knew he would do a good job.

As a friend and companion on desert trips or at sea, his local knowledge and his fascinating talk combined to make the journey enjoyable. He was well known to all the shaikhs and much respected everywhere. He had also become famous for his quiet unassuming generosity, giving aid to so many poor families, when he himself was only beginning to make money in sizeable amounts. When he became really old it was one of my greatest pleasures to spend an evening in Sharjah with him sitting on his tiny, shaky verandah which overlooked part of the market and the creek just beyond it. I would be enthralled and amused by his wonderful tales of the old days. Unfortunately the portable battery tape recorder only became available right at the end of his long life, and it is my constant regret that I was never able to tape his stories. His passing was a great loss to the community, but all who knew him thanked God for his life.

For me, those happy years on the Trucial Coast, spent in Dubai, Abu Dhabi and the hinterland, formed an interlude between our attempt to enter central and southern Oman in 1948–9 and the more elaborate expedition which was to set forth in early 1954. During this period, several things happened which altered the position as far as Company work in the area was concerned. The first was the formation by HMG in Sharjah in 1950 of a Levy Force, known to begin with as the Trucial Oman Levies, later to be renamed the Trucial Oman Scouts.

They started modestly with one British officer, from the Jordanian army, a small number of Arab officers and fifty non-commissioned officers and men, but within a few years they grew to the strength of a small battalion of nationals from the seven shaikhdoms. Lightly armed and mounted in Bedfords and Land Rovers, they soon commanded all the deserts of the coastal area, inland to the borders of Oman and to the oases of the al-Ain area. Their very creation produced an immediate improvement in the security of the area, particularly in the desert bordering Oman, and as they grew stronger and operated small armed patrols to the north and east, they were able to exert a pacifying influence on the tribes. This patrolling put an end both to bedouin raiding on the part of such tribes as the al-Rashid and the al-Afar, and to any resort to fighting in order to settle the quarrels of the tribes over rights to water, grazing and travel. What is more, they were able to achieve all this without any shooting. They worked skilfully and with patience.

Disputes continued over wells and grazing as they had done before the formation of the Levies, but instead of a dispute working up to a fight the

Levies would step in at the critical moment to gain a cooling-off period during which the shaikhs or the Political Agent, with the aid of the tribal leaders, could ensure a fair and open discussion of the problem; and this would usually, after much toil, lead to an acceptable solution; but many border questions remained unsolved. It was found essential in such cases to prevent the first killing of a tribesman which would start a feud which might last a long time. To advance from being an area in which one might almost expect trouble to being an area where one could go out into the desert assuming that there would be none, took a matter of perhaps three years. Abu Dhabi was, however, a special case since in that Emirate, after the ending of a Dubai-Abu Dhabi war in 1948, no insecurity at all was experienced. This was because of the effective control exercised by the Abu Dhabi shaikhs: the Ruler, Shaikh Shakhbut, on the coast and his brother, Shaikh Zayed, in the interior at al-Muwaiqi and al-Ain. We never needed guards in Abu Dhabi and travelled anywhere in those wide deserts without them. The beginning of an era of security in the hinterland of the Trucial Coast greatly facilitated oil company exploration, a considerable amount of which was done in the fifties and sixties, culminating in the finding of oil in Abu Dhabi in 1960. Dubai followed with the smaller sea-bed discovery in 1966.

A second important event was the occupation of the Omani village of Hamasah (also in the 'Buraimi' oasis on the Sultanate side) in the summer of 1952 by a small armed Saudi force who came in civilian clothes under the Emir Turki bin Ataishan, apparently at the invitation of the shaikh of the Al Bu Shams tribe in Hamasah, Rashid bin Hamad.

From 1935 to 1938, the Saudis had discussed with the British Government the claims which the Saudi king had made to the territories of both Abu Dhabi and the Sultanate, and agreement was almost reached on what became known as the Riyadh Line. However, final agreement on the details could not be reached and negotiations had lapsed by the time World War II broke out.

In 1949, ARAMCO, the American company which held the Saudi oil concessions, started sending out survey parties which made forays into Abu Dhabi territory, reaching even Khor al-Ghanadha near the Dubai frontier, where I bumped into them and talked to one of their party leaders who pretended he was lost. Later the Political Officer, Pat Stobart, met them when they were in company with a Saudi Emir in rather tense circumstances on Abu Dhabi territory further to the west.

The British Government complained, through diplomatic channels, to the Saudi Government about these intrusions. It was obvious that ARAMCO wanted Saudi boundaries to be extended, as their own concession to explore for oil and export it would be increased automatically to the same extent.

In April 1949, the Saudis had put forward claims to Abu Dhabi and Sultanate territory which far outreached their largest claims of the 1930s. No economic or political changes had taken place in the meantime to justify such a claim. Among other things, they laid claim to the Buraimi area, and consequently this affair, involving as it did a Saudi claim to two-thirds of Abu Dhabi's whole territory, has been known ever since as the Buraimi Dispute. In 1951, by the London Agreement, both sides (Britain and Saudi Arabia) contracted not to put forces into the disputed area. In January and February 1952, discussions took place in Dammam between the Saudi Government on the one hand and HMG on the other. HMG's representatives were assisted by the shaikhs of Abu Dhabi and Qatar (whose territory was also involved). No conclusion was reached. Later in 1952, Rashid bin Hamad, shaikh of the settled Al Bu Shams in Hamasah, went on the pilgrimage to Mecca and apparently, as we later discovered, agreed to a Saudi force coming to occupy his village. Saqr bin Sultan, shaikh of Buraimi village and paramount of the Naim, was also approached by the Saudis, but he would not agree to the Saudis entering Buraimi itself; thus the village which gave the dispute its name was not, ironically, itself directly involved in the subsequent Saudi occupation.

In the summer of 1952, in clear breach of the London Agreement, a small armed Saudi expedition went in motor vehicles from Dammam to Hamasah, crossing hundreds of miles of undisputed Abu Dhabi territory, to which the Saudis had laid no claim, in order to achieve its object. It is a reflection on the Saudi claim to this area as a part of Saudi Arabia that there never has been any sort of track or regular route, either for camels or cars, between Buraimi and Saudi Arabia. The Buraimi oasis is geographically part of Oman and Abu Dhabi, and before 1800 and after 1870 had no economic or social ties with Saudi Arabia. Once established again in Hamasah in 1952, the Saudis set up lines of communication with their homeland by sea but not through the port of Abu Dhabi, just as they had been forced to do when in occupation of Buraimi in the nineteenth century. The Sultan and the Imam of central Oman together gathered considerable irregular forces on the Batinah and in the Dhahirah. These would have proved overwhelming to the small Saudi group in Hamasah, but, wishing to avoid bloodshed, the British Government intervened to prevent fighting. First, there followed a Standstill Agreement in October 1952, and later in 1954 an Arbitration Agreement.

Thus, in 1953, at the time my Company was preparing a second major attempt at effective exploration in the search for oil in the interior of Oman, they found the entry blocked as the Saudis maintained a small police force of a commander and fifteen men encamped in the oasis area. Likewise, the Levies had a force of the same size under the terms of the arbitration agreement, but the Saudis and the Levies alike were supposed to be exerting no political influence outside the small camps which they occupied.

Strangely, although we subsequently had physical proof that they spent money lavishly, they made very little impression outside Hamasah village except at Dhank to the south, at Mahadah (the headquarters of Shaikh Obaid of the Bani Kaab), north-east of Buraimi in the Sultanate, and at al-Araqi, a village near Ibri also in Sultanate territory. They failed in the Abu Dhabi villages to persuade the people to change their allegiance.

For me, an interesting feature of the Saudi claims was a fascinating little view of the back-room boys at work. As an oil company official, I went over to Dhahran in 1951 to meet George Rentz of the ARAMCO research department. A scholar of the Arabic language, he had acquired a wonderful library and a very great knowledge of Saudi Arabia. When I called there, I found him busy attempting to stretch this knowledge into Abu Dhabi. He did not seem to realize before I came the kind of work I had been doing, and even after I told him I was of course careful to reveal nothing whatever of what we had learnt. He must have thought I was naïve and an innocent. He was confident of the justice of the Saudi case and was only too ready to explain it to me. I had just previously come across the Arabic version of a book of his called *The Eastern Reaches of Al Hasa*, which I had borrowed from a friendly Saudi. I had made copious notes on it and had guessed, and later determined, that it had been put together by the process of interrogating many bedouins at great pains in Dhahran. The results, as must be inevitable from such a process, were, to say the least, inaccurate.

Later the Saudis were to produce a memorial to support their case and, although many of what I regarded as the major inaccuracies of Rentz's book had by this time been corrected, the tribal information in the Saudi memorial seemed to me to be built upon similar inaccurate lines. The British Government, with the aid of the Abu Dhabi and Sultanate Governments, produced a more accurate memorial which, in my view, proved the opposite with finality. I was myself involved in collecting and gathering much of this information, important sections of which were provided by Julian Walker and Martin Buckmaster who both served many years as Foreign Office Political Officers in the area. The Saudi memorial was also subsequently spectacularly demolished by J.B. Kelly in his book *Eastern Arabian Frontiers*, using the results of his own deep research.

The memorial which the British Government produced contained a huge quantity of evidence concerning the case. It was based on a study of the people of these areas, their payment of taxes relevant to land ownership – water tax in al-Ain oases, tax on the setting up of fixed fish traps all along the coast to Qatar, taxes on dates and many other kinds of tax. It also quoted an extensive volume of documents showing that all government action taken as the result of a controversy or a crime or an incident in the Dhahirah and al-Ain area was dealt with by the Abu Dhabi and Sultanate officials, often acting together where the incidents concerned both countries as they so often did. This memorial is most impressive. It was based on a close study of tribal habit and movement.

As far as the Company's work was concerned the position which had been reached by 1952 was that, although the Trucial Coast remained geographically the best base for working southwards into the Omani deserts, the difficulties with the tribes in the northern Dhahirah and the presence of the Saudis in the oasis, which could only exacerbate the tribal problem, made any approach from the north unlikely to succeed for political reasons. The central mountain masif of Oman, and the fertile valleys which crossed it, stood between Muscat and the Omani desert; this area was, as we have seen, out of the direct administrative control of the Sultan's government based in Muscat and under that of the Imam. The Imam was opposed to Saudi intrusion and would co-operate with the Sultan on this, but he did not seem ready to co-operate on the subject of exploration for oil. This left the bedouin tribes, especially the Duru, who controlled the area which we wanted to explore, in a somewhat anomalous position in which they paid court, as they saw fit, both to the Sultan and the Imam. It was for this reason that it had become absolutely clear to us that an entry from the far south would be the only way in which we could get an exploration party into the field. This could not be done, however, until the Sultan had raised a mobile force to cover the security side. Naturally, and most important of all, he had also to obtain the consent of the bedouin tribes in the area.

After some time an agreement was reached with the Sultan to the effect that the Company's exploration party would land on the southern coast and reach the Fahud area from there to examine the formation which looked so promising from the air. In thus agreeing, the Company management in London, inspired I have no doubt by Dick Bird, took a courageous and imaginative step. They would be risking large amounts of money in an area of political doubt. Even if the oil was there, the risk was that they might never be able to operate for political reasons. I was away on a brief sojourn in Iraq when the agreement with the Sultan was finally reached, but I was told all about it when I returned to the Gulf.

Here I should describe briefly the geological aspect of our problem, since it was the geology which largely dominated our thinking in regard to entry into the Omani interior. I had spent a great deal of time out in the desert with geological parties. Sometimes I would write their notes as they dictated them, as we walked or scrambled. Being with them taught me to understand, if only in a simple-minded way, something of the matter. The Eastern Arabian peninsular is a sedimentary plateau, that is rock that had been laid down progressively on the sea bed as sediment. This may be suitable, when the age is right, both as source-rock, in which the marine matter is contained which turns into oil and gas, and as reservoir rock (not always or necessarily in quite the same place) which holds the deposit. The reservoir must have an impervious cap to withstand the pressure. The succession, that is the series of different rock strata, is about the same in Dhahran in Saudi Arabia as it is in Oman, and at all points in between. Thus all this sedimentary plateau is a possible prospect for oil. For oil to be capable of recovery it had to have been trapped and held under pressure. In this area this is commonly in an anticlinal or dome formation with impervious rock above and below. It may also be trapped in a fault and there are other possible rock formations, but in this area the anticline is the feature to look for. The top of this dome is often exposed and only partly eroded as a mountain or a hill. Some anticlines are hidden beneath a flat plane. Even good anticlines may have lost their oil through earth movements or other reasons.

I took a geological party once to the Seih Hatat in the interior only a few miles inland of Muscat. There the plutonic rock pushing up through the sedimentary has raised the latter and broken it leaving exposed cliffs where one can see on the cliff side the same geological succession as a drilling log in any well at Dhahran would show. The strata are all there in the same succession, wider or narrower perhaps, but basically the same. We, therefore, searched by air those desert areas which we could not as yet reach on the ground for the signs of anticlines or for any of the other structures which might be oil-bearing. Once found, these must be reached on the ground and first surveyed geologically to identify the age of the rocks. Then geophysical (seismic or gravity) surveys have to be run in order to give an underground picture of the rock formation. This tells you the shape of the formation, but one needs to know the geology of the area to interpret the seismic picture; then drilling sites can be chosen. Only drilling establishes whether oil is present and only test flow of the well establishes if it is in commercial quantity. Several wells may have to be drilled to assess a field properly. Thus we knew as a start that the whole area between Saudi Arabia and the volcanic uplift of the Oman mountains was an oil prospect; but all these processes, ending with drilling, had to be gone through before oil could be found. This explains why our air reconnaissance told us that Duru territory was the most interesting of all as seen from the air, and that Fahud looked the most favourable of all.

8

The Second Expedition

In early 1953 I was back in a bungalow in Bahrain. I was to replace Basil Lermitte as far as all concessions in the Gulf were concerned and, in particular, I was to work on the Oman project. I also had to continue to work on the gathering of information on the Buraimi problem in co-operation with HMG and the Gulf governments concerned. Plans for an expedition in Oman were coming to fruition. The Company had two aircraft in Bahrain which I could use whenever it was necessary. I could also make use of the comparatively new Gulf Aviation Service with its little Ansons (ex RAF) with fabric bodies.

Having seen the Batinah coast and explored some of the valleys inland of Muscat, parts of the Dhahirah plain and the Wadi al-Jizzi, I was beginning to know something of the Omanis and I came to like them very much. They are sturdy and intelligent and like most hill people, individualists. Their material surroundings were notable for what they lacked. The beautiful, but rugged and harsh scenery, the water and fertile soil of the valley bottoms were their only apparent physical assets. It was fascinating to think that such a lively people who had so little in the way of food or clothing or comforts might suddenly, through our efforts, enjoy the fruits of oil. Most of them had never seen a car or heard a radio; most had never known of tinned food; fresh food was severely limited in variety and quantity and they seldom were able to serve meat to their families. The simplest of our possessions were luxuries undreamt of to them; to modern medicine and modern science, they had no access. But I would add that they had a knowledge of human nature and also of simple, natural and effective cures for bodily ills, some of which seemed astonishingly effective, perhaps because the sufferers believed in them.

The urge to find the oil for which we were looking was strengthened for me and, I think, for one or two of my immediate colleagues in the

Company, as much on account of the benefit it would bring to the Omanis as for what it would bring to our very impersonal Company, whose shareholders were unknown and whose top management were no more than names to me. This was a natural emotion, and I say this without any wish to be thought either patronizing or self-righteous. It was exciting to be given the political responsibility in the field for such a venture, for something which might bring an abundantly rich future to people living in a totally impoverished area, with no other future visible for them. But if it was exciting when I thought of what there might be in front of us, it was rather depressing when I thought of the difficulties which then seemed to me insurmountable; and it was ironic that the very people who would be the ones to benefit seemed to present the main obstacle. The five years I had already spent on this project had been depressingly unsuccessful. Would the future be any better?

The Sultan of Oman had not yet raised the force which he regarded as essential. I was not yet in contact with the Duru; the attitude of the Imam was uncertain; the Saudis were to our north; no Western-type expedition had ever penetrated right into the interior. These were only some of our difficulties. The vital factor was to be the attitude of the Duru tribe towards our exploration of their lands. They were only partially within the sphere of influence of the Imam but, although they were not under the Imam's direct control, they were vulnerable to the other tribes of the interior since their date trees, which were all they had of any real estate, were in the towns and villages on the edge of the settled area, especially in Ibri and Tanaam. Their ownership of these trees was the vital point and the key to all that followed; it was a simple obvious point, but almost all the people involved managed to overlook it. In some cases I was glad they did so. Fortunately the Imam was old, not very active, and had no standing force of any kind and no administrative machine. We had every reason to expect that Shaikh Muhammad bin Abdullah of Ibri, who was closely related to the Duru, although not of their tribe, would help us, and if this proved to be the case the Imam might be in no position to thwart us. This is because Ibri was the key place on the edge of the desert which commanded the area of our oil operation.

I made many visits in 1953 to Muscat and far-off Salalah by light aircraft to see the Sultan and his officials. During this time, the Sultan was building up his mobile force and gathering information. The force was to be called the Muscat Field Force (the MFF). Many were the nights I spent at Salalah, the capital of Dhufar, either in the tiny RAF camp or in the Sultan's guest room before or after an interview with His Highness, who was spending almost all his time in that province. Dhufar is an attractive region. Strangely, the south-west monsoon, which blows from the beginning of June right through the summer, just catches the mountains of this corner of Arabia and precipitates a gentle rain for three months or more, and during this time the sun is hardly ever to be seen through the low cloud base. The result is that, unlike the remainder of the region, the southern slopes of the foothills and the plain of Salalah are lush green with long grasses and thick bush. On the coast, in place of the date palm of the Gulf, they grow the coconut with its tall, slender, shiny trunk, a pleasant contrast to eyes that are used to the rougher thicker date palm and its often dusty leaves. The Sultan's palace, right on the beach, was stoutly built of stone, with the roaring waves of the Indian Ocean seeming to pluck incessantly at its solid foundation, as if trying to drag it into the water. The palace interior, like that of the palace in Muscat, was immaculate, the staircase of slippery stone dangerously well polished. The Sultan had an obsession with clean floors. I once asked him how he kept them so shiny. 'I think you call it elbow grease,' he said with a smile and I believe he meant this literally.

Kindly in his attitude towards a visitor, the Sultan was a pleasure to meet, and I should have enjoyed these long talks by the window overlooking the roaring waves of the Indian Ocean much more if I had had more reason to believe that we should ever achieve what we were aiming at. I should also have felt more comfortable if I had not, by then, some idea of the nastier aspects of his rule. The Sultan spoke almost perfect English in a soft voice and had a great calm about him. He told me he was already forming a force of 400 men. This, he said, was a mystic figure in Omani battles. The leader who had 400 men would win; he would almost be allowed to win and probably without any need for fighting. Omani battles are fought according to conventions which I believe we have never tried to understand, and the Sultan may have been right when he said a force that numbered 400 would win. This was because in a country where the inhabited areas were split from each other by impassable mountains, where the only form of communication was on foot or animal back, where distances were great, and where there is no central administration and no standing force, it was both extremely difficult to gather an army and, once having gathered it, to maintain it as a cohesive force. The position was somewhat analogous to that of the Middle Ages in Britain, but in this case applied to a country that was divided by high mountains. The Sultan believed that if he could send in a force of this size and maintain it in the field by modern methods, especially if the Sultan's position became stronger financially and thus militarily, he must win. I think he was right provided he at the same time took positive steps to look after his people.

Circumstances were such that if I could not persuade him personally of my views, I had to accept the Sultan's decision and live with the consequences. But I saw the problems ahead of us rather differently from His Highness. Provided we could gain the support of the Duru and keep it, using a landing point in the south we could work at Fahud and at other sites in their area and find out whether or not oil was there. Once oil was found, then would be the time to worry about getting it out. There would then be money for the Sultan to extend his centralized administration over the whole of Oman, to raise a gendarmerie and create some structure of modern government. The area might (I supposed) have to be very gradually detribalized, and in the process the tribal chiefs kept in funds and their loyalty held. The Imam would have to be won over, but in view of his friendly attitude to the Sultan at the time of the Saudi occupation of Buraimi, this might not be difficult. These political issues were not of course for us to solve, but unless they were solved there would be no oil industry.

As we saw it the need was to land on the southern coast of the area at Duqm (a site chosen by our marine department), to gain the support of all the desert tribes and to advance inland to Ibri. It was essential to make sure of that town, to be certain that the Duru would not lose their vital palm trees to the control of the Imam, were the latter to attack Ibri. Ibri must not, therefore, remain as it were a marginal town vulnerable to the tribes which were closest to the Imam. For the preliminary landing we would need only a small force since the area was inhabited only by a few nomads. For the advance across the desert, likewise, a very small force of camp guards would suffice, but only providing the Duru were agreeable to our presence. For the final advance into Ibri we might need a larger force to ensure a bloodless entry to the town although we knew its shaikh to be loyal to the Sultan. The Shaikh of Ibri was also on the best of terms with the Duru as the shaikhly families of the two tribes had intermarried. The principal tribe in Ibri was the Yaaqib.

The Sultan was having difficulty in raising and training a force quickly, as he had virtually no sound basis on which to enlarge his small existing force as it lacked all the necessary training facilities from which to work. However, he was determined that when we landed in the south at the beach we had chosen, the whole force would be ready to land with us. It was the number of men that obsessed him. I explained that in my view it would be a mistake to concentrate so large a force on the beach in the early stages. We had little hope of finding water, there was no firewood, no shade and no material to make it, nothing on that barren shore. We would have to bring everything with us. The maintenance of 400 men on the beach posed an unnecessarily big problem. If the few tribesmen living in that area, of the Janabah tribe, were agreeable there would be no immediate security problem to face anyway. Above all it was the training of the force that mattered, not its numbers.

I argued that we would land with only a small force and then build up our base; and, in due course, when we had sufficient transport, petrol, water and stores ashore, advance into the centre of the Duru territory on the Wadi Amairi where there were good prospects of finding plentiful water. Then we could land more of the force if necessary and pass it through towards Ibri, using both Duqm and the Wadi Amairi area as our base camps, and thus avoid holding too many men at Duqm at any one time. I pleaded above all that we should have direct contact with the Duru and the Shaikh of Ibri as soon as possible. The Sultan agreed with me entirely on this last point, but time went by without any contact being made.

The Sultan's military advisers agreed with my thinking in regard to the troops, but the Sultan wanted it otherwise; he insisted in the first instance on landing all 400 men as quickly as we could, within a week or so, before doing anything else. Naturally, I reported my misgivings to my Company and, looking back on it, I see that I should have persuaded my Company by using stronger arguments and even greater emphasis that my plan was right and the Sultan's wrong, but the operation would then have been stopped. We would then have lost the money which the Company had been allocated from the groups which owned the Iraq Petroleum Company.

Despite all this, the Sultan's enthusiasm was infectious and, after all, we supposed he knew his country (I was constantly being told this by Company officials in London). I must confess the Sultan and the

Company carried me along with them on a road in which I myself had little trust.

Much of 1953 I spent in travelling between Bahrain, Qatar, Dubai, Muscat and Salalah. I was involved in study of the tribes and also in keeping track of the Sultan's military preparations, which by this time, after a false start, the Sultan had put in the capable hands of Colonel Percy Coriat, a British Officer of great experience who had formerly served in the Sudan and had newly entered the Sultan's service. But through no fault of his own he had no knowledge of Omani tribes and their history and never attempted to acquire it. Fortunately he accepted my advice on the political problems we faced.

While I was paying my visits to Muscat and Salalah, the Company was preparing ships, transport and stores for this quite elaborate and, by no means easy, operation. We had two naval-type vehicle landing craft and other smaller vessels including *Jamila* for the landing, and a fleet of six-wheeler Nubian load-carrying trucks, together with Dodges and Land Rovers as personnel carriers for the desert journeys. Our equipment included, in addition to tentage, a water-desalination plant, a generator and other quite heavy gear, as well as a mountain of tinned food and a huge load of petrol in metal cans (like the old jerrican).

All these preparations went on during the summer of 1953. I continued to press for contact with the Duru. Eventually, I was told that contact had been established, but I was unable to gain access to them myself, as I had wanted. This alleged contact appeared to have been made in the usual complex, uncertain and remote way I had begun to realize is customary in the tribal affairs of Oman.

At the last of my visits to the Sultan in Salalah, at which Major Chauncy the British Consul-General was present, the Sultan agreed to our entering the territory of all the tribes between the landing point Duqm and our objective Fahud. In February 1954, I was to go down by truck to meet the little oil company fleet, or that part of it which would sail from Muscat. There the soldiers would be embarked and all of us taken to the beaches at Duqm. Another landing craft was to come with supplies from Aden and would rendezvous with us off Duqm. It was the distinctly interesting situation in the interior that we sought to penetrate.

One bright February morning in 1954, I set off from Dubai by truck, reaching Muscat on the following evening. There I found the company and the advance party of the soldiers ready to sail. Before embarking I managed to see Sayyid Ahmad bin Ibrahim's secretary, Mahmud, who led me to believe that they still had not agreed our entry into their tribal area with the Duru shaikhs but would do so very shortly. As the Duru so seldom come to Muscat I was naturally very sceptical about the chance of Sayyid Ahmad's even seeing them, much less his obtaining their co-operation. This one factor could put in jeopardy the whole aim of the expedition: Fahud. With this gloomy news I went down to the foreshore where *Jamila*'s dinghy was waiting to take me out to her.

At this point, I had to say goodbye for a time, with much regret, to Sabir and Firdullah who were to go back to Dubai with the two trucks we had come down in. Land Rovers were already loaded on our ships (for the surveyor, the geologists and me), and we had to economize on staff as much as we could. This meant taking drivers only for the bigger trucks and driving the Land Rovers always ourselves. We had to watch the logistics problem very carefully on this operation. By late afternoon I was on board the Company vessel, the *Jamila*, a former wartime infantry landing ship. This was the same vessel I had sailed in earlier in the Gulf on survey work. Now she was loaded with stores and would also carry some of our personnel. Near us lay another Company vessel, the *Jasoura*, a vehicle landing craft which carried our vehicles.

We were to rendezvous at Duqm later in the week with the other similar ship chartered by the Company and likewise loaded with stores and vehicles. The beach had been chosen by air photography, but we would have to go ashore first in a small landing craft so that the ship's officers could check the beach profile before committing the vehicle landing craft to the landing. For myself the operation was all a bit reminiscent of Salerno and Normandy, but this time our aims were peaceful. Our General Manager, George Heseldin, who was responsible for all our Company's exploration, was on board, together with those Company officials who were in charge of the administration and logistics of this operation. Heseldin and the others wanted to see the landing, on which the Company had spent such a great deal of money, before returning by *Jamila* to Muscat and thence back to his headquarters in Tripoli, Lebanon. Also on board were Nick Fallon, our surveyor; Morton and McGinty, expedition geologists; Brown, a senior geologist; and three officers of the MFF, Colonel Percy Coriat, Mike O'Kelly and Frank Haugh.

We dined that night on *Jamila*'s deck. It was a lovely evening with not much wind and it was just the right temperature for sitting out of doors. The gaunt crags rose up on either side of us and the town, with only a few faint lights, lay in between them. In the moonlight we could see the patches of grey on the crags which showed where, over the years, the crews of visiting ships had painted their ship's name in white paint. There were hundreds of them, many dating back a long time; many were of the British frigates which had called there. Every ship seemed to have been in competition with her predecessors to get her name in a more prominent, more difficult position. Somewhere among them was HMS *Minerva* in which the young Nelson was serving as a midshipman in the late eighteenth century.

On *Jasoura*'s decks near us a hundred or so newly joined soldiers of the MFF were sitting, eating their evening meal. *Jasoura* was later to do further trips back to Muscat with another ship to pick up the remainder of what I called the 'Mystical Four Hundred'. Over dinner we discussed again points of detail in regard to the operation, and as we sat after dinner I felt I had to report what I had heard about the Sultan's failure to meet the Duru and how poor I thought the prospects for getting as far as Fahud might be, until this problem had been solved. Heseldin said, of course the object must be the Fahud area itself, but he was confident we should be there quite soon; I was being too pessimistic. I reiterated that I thought that the Sultan must be persuaded to get in touch effectively and quickly with the Duru and this was the point we must get over to him when we met him at Duqm, where he said he hoped to meet us later.

I also feared that the arrival of the expedition on the coast would in itself arouse the antagonism of the Imam. I doubted if he would do more than complain, as he could do nothing to oppose such a landing physically; but the danger of his then using our arrival to influence the Duru against the Sultan (if he could reach them first) was one we could not disregard. If that happened, our chances of getting inland would virtually disappear, and Oman might break up into a series of small and unrecognized states. Political instability of this kind would prevent any company searching for oil, perhaps for many years to come.

Percy Coriat largely agreed with my argument. He was, he said, very worried about his force. The men had been recruited in far too great a hurry without the necessary training facilities and he had no properly equipped base; he had no cadre of Arab officers and NCOs to draw on; but he did have three British officers, on contract to the Muscat government, who had retired from the British Army. He also had a group of Adenis who had seen some service in the Aden Levies, and he planned to use these as his non-commissioned officers, but they were out-of-work soldiers of fortune without much training and it was already evident that they did not get on well with the Omani troops. Even without any enemy to bother him, Percy thought he would have difficulty with his own force. His views on his own troops were reminiscent of Wellington's famous comment before Waterloo. I hoped this was a good omen. He smiled when I pointed this out. Moreover, he did not yet have an effective organization to back him logistically. He was short of equipment and he had very little qualified administrative staff. It was, he thought, ludicrous to field a force of this kind in this manner.

To begin with, the Company would have to give vehicles to him in order to carry the force inland. This was accepted by the Company for as long as he was awaiting his own transport, which was on order; and until it came he would have to rely entirely on us logistically whether at Duqm or inland. This in itself he found most unsatisfactory. So did we. Heseldin said that it was too late to hold up this operation; we had to do the best we could with things as we found them. For practical reasons the weather demanded that we start work before the onset of the hot season, and, even more important, before the monsoon in May, which might close the beach-head for at least three months, when high seas and frequent severe dust storms were predicted.

He ended the discussion by saying once again that the Sultan obviously knows his own country best, and he was confident he would be proved right. We were not to worry about the effectiveness, or lack of it, of the MFF. The Sultan did not want to achieve our common aim by means of physical force and certainly had no intention of fighting, otherwise we should not have gone along with him. He agreed that with the bedouin some show of strength might be needed, but just the presence of troops was all that would be required. After Heseldin had left us to go to his cabin, Percy and I, who would later sleep on the deck, went on talking. Percy said he had been so preoccupied with the difficulty of raising this force in a few short months, that he had not had the opportunity to study the political position. He was, after all, a newcomer to the area. It looked to him as if, on top of what had seemed almost insuperable difficulties on the military side, he now had to face problems of even greater complexity politically. However, he remained cheerful, pulled my leg about being a Cassandra and said we must look on the bright side; after all a miracle might happen.

I was naturally very pleased with this attitude. I had had some chances to talk with Percy on my previous visits to Muscat since his arrival but, as he said, he had then been so preoccupied with the problem of raising a force out of apparently nothing and with very little time to do it in, that we had not discussed in enough detail the political background which was all new to him. This was really the first good opportunity we had had to talk about the political problems and for me to brief him at all. It was difficult to explain the position to anyone with no experience of Oman and with no knowledge of the tribal names. The political position, as far as the Oman government was concerned, had never been made fully clear by the Sultan, even to me, and it was not until the very last moment before we went aboard that I finally learned that the Sultan still had been unable or unwilling to do anything about the Duru on the lines I had suggested.

Percy was an impressive figure, tall, lean, and tough, with a black patch concealing the loss of an eye as a result of a war wound. He had a handsome, prominent nose and a thin weathered face. He looked the part of a colonel who had had years of hard service in tropical countries behind him. Much of this service had been in the Arabic-speaking parts of the Sudan and he was familiar with the language and quickly adapted himself to the local dialect. That night I went to bed on *Jamila*'s deck, my mind full of anxiety. However, I hoped to see the Sultan on the beaches at Duqm, which he planned to visit by sea from Salalah some time, after we had landed. I could at least discuss it all with him then, putting forward my recommendations yet again. It had been nearly two months since I had last seen him.

On the following day, we put into the port of Sur to pick up Shaikh Salim bin Nasir, the paramount shaikh of the Janabah tribe, a section of which frequented the Duqm area in the autumn, winter and spring. Salim had his instructions from the Sultan but he did not know exactly when we would come to pick him up, and there was no way in which we could have told him, as there was no speedy communication out of Muscat to other towns. We already had with us two government representatives who were supposed to help us with tribesmen whom we met ashore, but I soon found that they knew very little about the tribes and nothing whatever of the geography of southern Oman. They reminded me of Yusuf who had been with us in the Wadi al-Jizzi. They were not influential people and they would not, I thought, be any use; but I counted on Salim to help us, at least in regard to any of his own people whom we came across, and as a paramount shaikh of a major tribe, he was a man of importance.

I did not expect to find the Janabah in very large numbers ashore at Duqm. They would, I was told, be friendly and I did not expect any difficulty with bedouin at the landing point, but there could be difficulties when we struck inland to the north into al-Wahibah country since the latter are not on good terms with the Janabah, and we had no representative from the al-Wahibah with our party. The Muscat government had either failed to produce one or, perhaps rightly, felt that to have one alongside Salim might have been awkward for us. The tribes were not actually at feud, just rather 'unfriendly' I was told and, in these circumstances, we felt we should have had a representative from both. I had done much the same elsewhere when I had been with tribes which were mutually unfriendly and, by having leaders from both with me, had got away with it. We should also meet another tribe, the Harasis. They were a small tribe who were on terms with the Janabah and I did not expect any difficulty with the few whom we were likely to come across.

We sailed well before dawn and, early the following morning, we put in at the port of Sur. I had one of the Janabah with me and he and I were to go ashore to pick up Shaikh Salim bin Nasir and one or two followers. 'Mind it is only one or two,' were my instructions from Heseldin, and 'We sail at four.' 'More like fifteen or sixteen and sailing tomorrow,' commented Percy Coriat sardonically. I thought he was right and, after all, it is hardly reasonable to arrive so suddenly and ask people to pack up and come with you at a few hours' notice. Shaikh Salim would be justified if he asked for more time but Heseldin would never be made to see this.

Percy said he was particularly interested to see Sur, since it was the place where the British-Indian Army landed in 1820 and 1821, after which they attacked the tribes in the hills inland and a whole brigade of British-Indian troops under British officers were cut to pieces. 'Not,' he said firmly, 'that I think anything like that will happen to us.' It took us some time to walk to Salim's house and we arrived only to find he was out. We eventually ran him to earth in another house and managed to persuade him to go back to his own, after having coffee. Once we reached his house he disappeared from our view while we were entertained to coffee. Percy was amused by all this and prophesied that we should be kept waiting the rest of the day. Whilst we were waiting for Salim, we took a short walk along the waterfront. Sur is not a very beautiful town. The main part of it, where the Janabah live, is on the peninsula which guards the entrance to the extensive but rather shallow creek. This part of the town is almost flat and, since there is a very poor water supply in the town itself, it has no gardens or trees and the low, flat-roofed houses have a singularly colourless, unattractive air.

Sur was a considerable port for country-craft and for the large sailing ships (called *booms*), partly powered, that went as far as Zanzibar in one direction and Kuwait in the other. There were a number of wooden ships, berthed and pulled up on the beach of the creek. Some were under repair and boats were being built at the water's edge. I walked a little way up a small hill hoping to catch sight of Bilad al-Sur, the inland part of the town, which is well watered and has extensive gardens, but I was unable to see it and we did not have time to walk further; I had no adequate map to see how far away the gardens were. All the water for the port of Sur is brought on the backs of animals from Bilad al-Sur, I suppose two miles or more away.

On the far side of the creek is Ayqa where the Bani Bu Ali live, but we had no reason to go near them since they do not visit any of the country our expedition was planning to explore. This is a section of the famous Bani Bu Ali tribe, the bulk of which live inland of Sur, who overcame the British-Indian brigade of which Percy had spoken. In turn, they were defeated a year later with great loss, and paradoxically have always been reckoned to be very friendly disposed towards the British in consequence, but we did not have a chance to test this.

Salim did his best to make us stay for a late lunch; it was already after three in the afternoon. He wanted to bring about twenty tribesmen with him and a great deal of kit, but he was persuaded eventually to cut it down to six and a good deal of kit, despite the fact that I had explained that we had in the ships sufficient tentage, bedding, food and cooking utensils to make them all very comfortable. We finally got all this gear down to the beach and put it on board the waiting motor launch. When we reached *Jamila* it was already five, but Percy thought we had done very well to bring only so few so quickly.

Salim proved very pleasant although a bit fussy and I felt I could rely on him when dealing with his own people. He was sure he could also get us through the Duru area, but I thought it might well turn out that he could not, as his tribe and the Duru were known to be on bad terms. This is in marked contrast to Wilfred Thesiger's experience when he used Janabah to get him through Duru country. This was several years earlier and the shaikh concerned was a different one. He was Yasir, I think, the real paramount of this scattered tribe. Heseldin asked him just this question and, with me interpreting, he heard Salim's confidentially affirmative reply. 'There you are; your fears are groundless,' I was told. Heseldin wanted to visit the curious nearby harbour of Khor al-Jaramah that evening but it was now too late in the day to negotiate the entrance. *Jamila* stood off the coast and waited until first light when we turned towards this most unusual waterway.

Ras al-Hadd is the easternmost point of Arabia; near this point there are three interesting creeks, one at Sur, another about twelve miles to the east, called Khor al-Jaramah, and, just beyond it, Khor al-Hajar, right on the tip of Arabia. Early next morning we sailed towards the shore. The entry to Khor Jaramah was difficult, but fortunately the tide was slack as *Jamila* sailed into the narrow twisting entrance with the rocks close to us on either side. Once inside the channel, it opened up suddenly to an extensive creek over two miles long and more than a mile wide with deep water inshore to the north.

We spent about an hour exploring it; there was no sign of human habitation and it seemed to us that it was a very fine harbour going to waste. It might be useful later. According to Salim, the reason for its disuse is that there is no fresh water within reach of it. If there had been, the port of Sur would surely have been built there instead, since it is a far finer harbour than Sur's own shallow creek. One wonders why it is not now developed. We sailed out again and passed by the entrance to Khor al-Hajar but we did not go into that creek since the entry to that large but shallow inlet was not deep enough for a vessel as big as *Jamila*. We still had plenty of time in hand and two days later in the evening we made our rendezvous with the other ships off Duqm and there we anchored for the night.

9

The Landing and a Setback

I was up at first light the following morning and from *Jamila*'s deck saw that the two vehicle landing craft had anchored just off the shore beside us. We lowered into the water our very small assault landing craft, which we carried on the after deck. It was arranged that a small party of soldiers with Percy Coriat, Salim bin Nasir, Heseldin and myself would go ashore first in this small boat. As we were making these preparations, we were astonished to see five sailing boats being launched from the beach. A number of people climbed into them, put the sails up and came straight out towards us. Before we could get our motorboat ready with its little party, the five sailing boats sailed right through our fleet without apparently giving us a look. I naturally asked Salim what it was all about and he replied perfectly calmly, 'Oh they are going fishing. They do that every morning this time of year.' Never before in recorded history had such a landing been made on this wild and barren coast and yet this was the remarkably cool reaction of the only inhabitants.

In front of us, to the left, was a low cliff jutting out to sea, ending in a pointed rock; inland the ground rose to perhaps a hundred feet, but it looked higher. The escarpment then ran back inland leaving a sandy bay behind which were low dunes dotted with stumpy trees. We could make out a few people on the foreshore and one or two small sailing boats and dug-out canoes drawn up on the sand, but we could see no huts or tents. Smoke was rising in the area of the stumpy trees and this must be where the Janabah fisher-folk lived. We climbed aboard our little assault landing craft and were soon chugging through a fairly calm sea to the shore. We drove hard up on to the beach, after the manner of landing craft, and being well used to this I was hanging on as tightly as I could, ready for the sudden stop. Heseldin and Percy Coriat were standing on the half-decked stern and quite what happened I did not see, but

Heseldin fell overboard with a splash and Percy just saved himself at the last moment. Heseldin claimed Percy pushed him but the latter denied this. However, no damage was done and we all got ashore dry except for Heseldin who had seen nothing at all amusing in this little incident.

Percy was soon marching about with his long ash stick which he always carried, flicking the dust into the air to see how the wind took it and looking for a suitable place to put his tents away from the worst dust. The motorboat went back with a message to the others that all was well ashore for the main landing operation to start and perhaps, even more important, for a change of clothes for Heseldin. Meanwhile, in another small boat the ship's officers were taking soundings and examining the approaches to the beach at three chosen points for the vehicle landing craft.

Salim and I walked through the soft sand to where the bedouin were. We spent some time talking to them and I was astonished how calmly they had accepted our arrival. They saw nothing remarkable in it. Later in the morning our three ships weighed anchor and steamed in abreast; each made a successful landing about one hundred yards apart and got their doors down on to the dry sands of the beach. It was a perfect landing place. Out came the men and the first of the vehicles. Unloading proceeded until the tide began to turn and the ships pulled off to return to complete unloading on the high tide the next day. As soon as my Land Rover was ashore, I went for a tour in it with Salim and some of his men. We went first to Nafun, a tiny encampment where it was hoped to base the MFF, since there was brackish water which the bedouin stoically drink; this would at least serve us all for washing, even if we were not tough enough to drink it. There we found a small encampment of Janabah. They greeted Salim warmly, but again expressed little surprise at our arrival.

This section of the Janabah was a strange group based on distant Sur where they owned palm trees and houses. The tribesmen spent some of their time, especially in autumn and winter, on the coast in the Nafun area fishing. They also grazed camels there. Some travelled there by camel, some by small boat, usually remaining until just before the monsoon and the dust storms, which made living in that area almost impossible for most of the summer, as we were to discover for ourselves later. Others of the Janabah lived permanently in Sur town and others again in central Oman. All together they were a very large tribe.

At Nafun the escarpment comes almost to the sea and there is a small plain covered with thorn and other small trees between it and the water. The sand is light-coloured and very fine, in many places just dust, the trees gaunt and scraggy and the whole of this coast has a depressing, almost lunar landscape. The Janabah lived in harsh conditions; they simply placed their few belongings under trees in wooden chests and they also used more fragile boxes, placed vertically against the diminutive trees, looking rather like small wardrobes, for storage of some of their equipment. They lived entirely in the open with only small pieces of cloth two or three feet square stretched between the branches of the trees to give some shade from the sun. In winter the sun was warm but the air cool and it was cold at night. In summer it would be intensely hot, but from May to August the monsoon would blow strongly up the coast from the south-west and this, we were told, produced thick sandstorms which would blanket the place for days or even weeks at a time. The severity of these storms, the bedouin said, varied from year to year. They were the main cause of the movement of almost all the nomad inhabitants northwards to Sur during this period.

I spent the afternoon visiting the few encampments which we could find, talking, joining them over their coffee, making friends and offering the men work. We had brought some labourers with us but we naturally wanted to employ some of the people of the region if we could. However, as we had rather expected, they did not seem at all anxious for manual work in our camps and, apart from half a dozen guides whom Salim chose, we could not engage anyone. I tasted the water at Nafun well and found it just drinkable; by itself it was pretty horrid, but as water for tea and coffee, it was just possible. It was no worse than Tobruk water, which the British Army used to rely on during the war in Cyrenaica. However, we had the distillation units with us on which we planned to rely for drinking purposes. Salim then showed me a remarkable thing about his people. He pointed to a large chest by one of the encampments. It had a series of concentric rings round it in the sand, made by a stick. Salim said it was the custom that if these rings were there, the chest and its contents would be safe. In the winter the sand or dust was stable enough for the rings to remain for many months and Salim said that a chest so marked and left unattended would never be tampered with. Whether the basis of this was superstition I could not find out, but such was the practice of his tribe.

We got back to camp to find tents already pitched and a meal being cooked. The distillation plant was working and the electric generator was making power. Nick Fallon, our surveyor, had been up to the escarpment towards the south-west in a Dodge Power Wagon and said that a very little work would make a track for our vehicles up on to the plateau. He confirmed reasonably firm going on top of the scarp. Percy Coriat had put up his camp near the Company one, but was prepared, when more vehicles came, to move the main body to Nafun, a place he aptly named 'No Fun'.

Heseldin departed with the ships when they had been unloaded, leaving me with instructions to press on to Fahud, instructions which I knew and he knew I could not fulfil unless I persuaded the Sultan to permit us to go. The two larger ships were to return to us with the remainder of the troops and this, after a week, they accomplished. We had to await the arrival of the Sultan by sea from Salalah before we could go very far inland or into Duru country. In the following weeks Nick Fallon and the geologists went out on survey expeditions, keeping to the south of the roaming grounds of the Duru. I used to accompany them to begin with in case they met any bedouin; but we established before long that the Jiddat al-Harasis, which is a large stony plateau south and west of our camp, stretching towards Dhufar province, was almost un-inhabited at that time of year and there was no need for me to be with them. We met only a handful of the Harasis on these journeys and they were very friendly. We cleared a suitable area to land our small Company aircraft. We now had de Havilland Doves.

These expeditions were the first of their kind in that part of Arabia and, other than the camel treks of Wilfred Thesiger and Bertram Thomas, we knew of no other foreign explorers who had visited this region; as we had the maps of the journeys of the two who had, we could be certain that on most of our trips we were the first foreigners ever to have visited many of the areas. Only the bedouin of two or three tribes ever travelled there. We navigated by sun and prismatic compass but could always find our way back without navigation, simply by following our own tracks: there were no others.

Nick Fallon, being a surveyor, did much of our navigation, but when I was without him I used a rod which I had brazed vertically on to the bonnet of my Land Rover as a sun compass. You have to set the car in the required direction with a prismatic compass, held well away from it, mark the shadow of the rod made by the sun with your dampened finger in the dust on the bonnet and keep on that line. You must make a fresh mark every half-hour or so. In flat country this gives a very accurate course. In dunes it is all much harder, as it is with any kind of compass in a vehicle. I had operated like this during the war in Egypt.

We used to spray our trucks with anti-fly spray soon after leaving Duqm and we knew we should not see another fly until we got back, although there were clouds of them at Duqm itself once our camp had been established, despite our constant efforts to kill them. On such trips we took no tents but allowed ourselves the luxury of either camp beds or air mattresses and, to pitch camp, we simply put these between the stationary vehicles. Our only discomfort was the cold at night and sometimes the mist. One would wake up in a misty sunlight to find the person sleeping nearest to you was out of sight in the swirling white clouds of fog and these might not clear until the sun had been up for an hour or more.

We had to await the Sultan before attempting a deeper foray into the desert towards Fahud, as Percy had orders not to move until he came. Meanwhile I applied myself to the intractable tribal problem which might prevent our penetration into the interior. We had with us the two Sultanate officials whose job was to help me with any tribes, other than the Janabah, whom we might bump into, but they were unable to help me until I could find any bedouin for them to talk to. Whether their presence then helped or not I could not tell, as all the bedouin we met were friendly. The first of these inland tribes, the Wahibah, as I have said, were on bad terms with the Janabah and we restricted our activities at the outset to Janabah and Harsusi country along the coast. I managed to make contact myself with the Wahibah whose nearest encampments were rather uncomfortably close, to our north. They accepted our presence and gave due respect to the representatives of the government, but they said if we wanted to work in their area we should have to give up using Salim and our Janabi guides while in their tribal districts. To this I naturally agreed and promised to employ their guides.

The Sultan himself visited us by sea from Salalah in HMS *Flamingo*, a Royal Navy frigate stationed in the Gulf. He had with him Major Chauncy who was British Consul General in Muscat. He landed in a small boat and inspected the troops. He expressed himself disappointed in them. 'They are only boys,' he said in disgust. Percy felt he had to agree. I pointed out yet again during a long conversation which I had with the Sultan that on this coast the troops were unnecessary anyway. Fahud could only be reached by agreement of the Duru where only a few guards if any might be needed. Some of the 400 men I thought might well be needed later in the Ibri area if we ran into armed opposition.

The Sultan would still not listen to my reasoning. He again made promises that the Duru would be contacted and in the meantime restricted us to an area of the coast and the Jiddat al-Harasis, putting this in writing in a long letter to me, which he wrote on board the frigate, in his excellent English with his own neat and clear hand. This letter was sent ashore only just before the frigate sailed. To my thinking the letter meant an end to all our hopes at least in the near future. It was the most disappointing letter I think I have ever received, and it read as follows:

HMS *Flamingo* at sea
18 March 1954

CONFIDENTIAL

Dear Mr Edward Henderson,

Because of several interviews I had yesterday and various subjects which I discussed with different persons, it had totally slipped out of my mind to take into consideration what the Commandant Lt Col Coriat informed me about the force and its present strength when I, Major Chauncy, the Consul General and yourself discussed the limit of the area which your geologists might explore, and that was just before the ship sailed from Ras Duggam.

The Commandant informed me that there is still quite a number of men who he considers are not fit to be retained as soldiers and might be discharged. Thus the strength of the force will still be reduced whereby it will make it impossible for your geologists to penetrate inland as I told you in the presence of Major Chauncy and I regret very much to tell you this after re-considering the whole matter and I am sure this is well understood by all as I have on several occasions informed everybody concerned that no penetration from the beach-head should take place unless we had the full force. Now the force has been considerably reduced and still it will be reduced before we can get replacements. I regret I do not see my way to agree to your penetration at present to the whole limit which we discussed yesterday until we have the full force at the beach-head. However, with present force in hand I still agree to your geologists exploring the following places but under no circumstances should they go beyond this limit.

1) Duggam and its immediate surroundings to Nafun, Sai and Bai but not to Saraib and up to Khaluf or al-Hugf.

2) Jiddat al-Harasis to Tarafa on the boundary between Dhofar province and al-Jaddah (Sharbatat to 55° and 20° in the north).

I must say the force has been formed in a hurry and without thinking of other problems and as we all must know that this being so things are apt to turn like this.

Really there is much to be said about the whole affairs from what I have seen and heard during my very short visit to Duggam but I shall stop my pen here with a wish that things may be worked out satisfactorily.

I am informing Major Chauncy that I have written this letter to you so that there should be no misunderstanding on the sbject.

Please telegraph to me just saying that you have received this letter to you by HMS *Flamingo*. I have requested the Commander of the Ship to see that this letter reaches you safely to which he very kindly agreed to do so.

Yours sincerely,
Said bin Taimur

PS I should like to urge your company to improve the water problems as there are complaints about this. They should make vigorous search for finding adequate supply of water for all purposes.

(Signed) Said

He could hardly have made his point clearer. It was typical of him that he put his crippling limitation on our exploration only after he had left us, sending the information to me when he knew it would be too late for me to reply. I wondered what Heseldin would make of this restriction which I reported to him by letter on the first Company aircraft that visited us. The reductions in the force to which the Sultan referred in his letter had been made by Percy Coriat. Some men he regarded as unfit or too young, and he sent all the Adeni non-commissioned officers away because they got on badly with the soldiers. He was thus left with no junior leaders save only those few whom he had promoted already from the Omani recruits.

We soon established an airstrip on the escarpment, our landing craft made further trips and then returned to their normal duties, and logistically the expedition was now firmly based. We later heard that the Imam formally complained to the Sultan about the Duqm landing, but he did nothing else about it. It was clear that politically we were reaching a stalemate, and I advised my Company in this sense. The Company, however, still believing our General Manager, Heseldin, rather than me, was confident that things would soon turn out as we all wished.

There was little I could do at Duqm where the survey continued in the limited southern area, and after the first two months I returned to Bahrain. From there I revisited Muscat, by light aircraft, to try to urge the Omani authorities to make direct contact with the Duru. Sayyid Ahmad said he had no authority to do this, and the Sultan was still in far-off Dhufar and did not want to talk further about it, although Sayyid Ahmad and His Highness were in direct daily communication by radio. He said a visit by me to the Sultan would not be well received. I also paid visits by air to Duqm where survey work was continuing without interruption in the limited area permitted.

Late in the spring of 1954, I heard the news that the old Imam, Muhammad bin Abdullah al-Khalili, had died in Nizwa and that the paramount shaikhs of the Hinawi and Ghafiri factions had, on their own initiative, 'elected' Ghalib bin Ali al-Hinai as his successor. From the story that filtered through, this did not seem as if it had been a widely accepted election, more a choice by the two key shaikhs, but there had been no actual resistence so far to the new Imam. This would mean that the people of the mountain would accept him. It then became clear that Ghalib himself was little more than a front for his tougher and more ambitious and effective brother, Talib bin Ali.

Talib's policy soon became evident. He wanted to tear up the Sib Agreement and carve out a separate state for himself in the interior. As we have seen, the old Imam had complained at the Duqm landing and took no action other than this, but Talib now began to raise the tribes and recruit an army. He toured the immediate area of Nizwa with this army to consolidate his position, but our information was that this activity was unpopular among the shaikhs and tribesmen alike. His 'army' (merely armed irregulars) lived on the land and paid for nothing. I was told that the individual shaikhs of the various tribes, who resented being forced to feed his army, felt their positions were being eroded; the Sib Agreement had allowed them much authority, and they wished to keep it that way. Talib also made his brother's faction unpopular by imposing a draconian tax on 'luxuries'. How in such an area, without an administration, it was to be collected was baffling, and I am sure it never was systematically gathered in, and I wondered what in that country at that time could really be called a luxury other than the locally made jewellery. All the signs pointed to a very fluid and uncertain situation in the interior and to the possibility that if Talib could get a grip on the tribal leaders of the Duru and the shaikhs of Ibri, any chance at all of our getting into Fahud would finally disappear.

In June the Imam and Talib threatened Ibri. This was a development of immediate major importance to us. The Duru made a living in their wide desert lands by digging and carrying salt, making and carrying charcoal and by breeding and selling their camels. They also collected sulphur used in making gunpowder locally. This is how they made their wealth which they invested in trees in the date gardens of their village Tanaam, only seven miles from Ibri and in Ibri itself. They owned some property, mainly trees, in other towns that bordered the desert. For this reason, whoever held Ibri and Tanaam controlled the Duru. Ibri was ruled by the shaikh of the sedentary Yaaqib tribe, Muhammad bin Abdullah, who was on close terms with the Duru with whom his family had intermarried. From 1925 to 1952 there had been a *wali* or governor in Ibri paid by the Imam, but in the last two years Ibri seemed to have swung towards the Sultan; and the Duru respected the power both of the old Imam and of the Sultan.

In the summer of 1954 the situation in inner Oman again changed rapidly. Fortunately, by this time the Company had established a representative in Muscat so that as the news trickled through he was able to cable me whether I was in Bahrain (which was our concessionary headquarters), Qatar (where we had our exploration headquarters), or Duqm itself, which I visited when I could.

This involved me in a series of flights, usually in a Dakota to Duqm or in a Dove to Muscat. Muscat as we have seen had a poor airstrip at Bait al-Falaj. It was a strip I knew only too well since I spent two days with fifty workmen clearing it in 1948 for the first aircraft, a Rapide, to land there since the war. Our pilot declared that although it was rather too soft they thought it a reasonable risk in a Rapide or a Dove, provided you took off towards the sea regardless of which way the wind was blowing. Taking off inland in a piston-engined aircraft was dangerous, and the last one to try it, in 1945, an RAF Dakota, had crashed. Even going out towards the sea meant taking a twisting course immediately after take-off, down the valley with the rocks too close to the wingtips, but one got used to it. (Later in the decade the strip was tarmacked, and it then became quite safe for small jet aircraft such as the BAC 111 which climbs so much more steeply, but even in a jet aircraft some passengers may have felt a certain concern.)

The trip to Salalah, which I made so many times, but which was barred to me now, was an easy one except between June and September when the monsoon clouds were down at 400 feet. We would refuel at Masirah and my favourite pilot Captain Wolf would follow the coastline at the level of the bottom of the clouds (about 400 feet) until he came to the Sultan's palace when he would turn right and land. Other pilots would fly at 10,000 feet and let down to the radio beacon, hoping to cross the coastline below 400 feet when they could see the palace and land on the strip. That was 'standard' procedure. Captain Wolf felt that the standard procedure was dangerous as the mountains rise to 6,000 feet inland of the airstrip and, if you were to miscalculate, you would fly right into them. His own technique seemed to be perfectly safe, but it was uncomfortable when we were following a low cliff edge in a high wind producing considerable turbulence, and the last hour in was very uncomfortable indeed. However, if I sat in front, which I normally did, since the pilot had no co-pilot, I felt quite happy, as I could see. In the cabin behind I would feel awful.

Duqm in the summer presented an even worse difficulty because of the sandstorms. These storms were extraordinary in their severity. For example, during a visit I made there in early June, I went early one morning in a Land Rover the four miles from our camp to the airstrip to meet an aircraft taking a radio transmitter with me. Just as it was due to arrive and we had made radio contact with the pilot, the wind started to blow hard and the sand came up like a blanket. The radio went dead. I never saw or heard the aircraft itself. The pilot told me later that on approaching he had made out the airstrip, but it had at once been blotted out by blowing sand and he returned to Qatar from where he had come. My companion and I meanwhile had got into the Land Rover and closed it down as much as possible. By this time we could not see the front edge of the bonnet from the steering wheel, and there we stayed all day long, half suffocated in dust and heat, until the wind abated and visibility improved sufficiently to enable us to return to camp, as the sun was setting. This kind of storm was repeated, and the duration of each one grew longer until survey work based on Duqm had to be suspended. But we were just able to keep the camp open through the summer.

We received good news in June that the Duru shaikhs had come of their own accord into Muscat. The Company immediately, at my request, gave me an aircraft, and I went down to see them. Sayyid Ahmad had arranged meetings for me with Shaikh Muhammad Said Tina, the aged paramount of the Duru, and his son Matar, in Ahmad's private house which was built into the town wall by the main gate of Muscat. These meetings were usually in the afternoon and Sayyid Ahmad served us from a very English looking tea tray, and we sat on rather splendid looking and genuine Victorian armchairs. The old paramount would soon get tired of the chair and prefer to sit on the floor. After the first meeting, it was clear, both to Sayyid Ahmad and myself, that we had reached the critical moment. If we dealt adequately with the shaikhs, the Duru would remain loyal to the Sultan and allow the Company to do their exploration. If they went away dissatisfied, they would immediately make their peace with Talib and the new Imam, Ghalib.

Knowing full well that the Sultan would not agree I had nevertheless brought with me enough cash to satisfy the shaikhs and this I was proposing to give them strictly as a payment for their services, for their travel and their work as guides in the forthcoming expedition. I had a long conversation with Sayyid Ahmad about this, and he said that he realized that this sum must be paid, but he did not want to know about it officially and he would be looking the other way when it was done. So, we had the bizarre experience, at our third meeting, of Sayyid Ahmad taking the old man into a corner of the room and sitting and talking to him on the floor, while I sat next to the shaikh's son, Matar, handing him the money under the tea table in a large sealed envelope. 'For services rendered and to be rendered,' I said in a whisper. I just prayed that the Sultan in far-off Salalah would never hear of it, and that this might prove to be the decisive moment.

We then resumed our conversation among the four of us. It was agreed that the Duru shaikhs would come to Muscat by mid-September, and I would take them on from there to Duqm, where we would go with a party of geologists into the Fahud area. It was also agreed that were the Imam to attack Ibri or Tanaam in the meantime the shaikhs would come immediately to me at Sharjah. This was because they might not find it easy, or even possible, to go to Muscat through the mountains (where the Imam would have control), and it would be safer for them to come up to al-Ain where they could hire a truck to get them to Sharjah. We thought it unwise to attempt the expedition before September because to take large numbers of men into the area in the middle of the summer would be risky.

Our last Victorian tea party went off very successfully, and I left Sayyid Ahmad's house in a much more hopeful mood. At the party, Sayyid Ahmad asked if I would be making one of my visits to the Sultan and he recalled in detail my description of the uncomfortable flight which was entailed in a summer visit. He recommended that I should take note of the bad weather and refrain from a visit. This, I took as more than just a hint that he himself would not be telling the Sultan our story, and I left with his firm agreement that I could tell the Company to plan an expedition to Fahud in September. I so reported to the Company which made preparations accordingly. When I reported this favourable turn inevitably Heseldin said 'I told you so.' I suppressed my irritation as well as I could. Sayyid Ahmad had also agreed, at my request, that I should have the assistance of Shaikh Sultan bin Seif al-Hawsini, who was the paramount Shaikh of the Hawasinah and highly respected by all the tribes concerned. He would not quite be an official representative of the government, I was told, 'but he would be there to help'.

Messages continued to come up from Muscat after I got back to Bahrain, which caused us to postpone our expedition until mid-October, when I was promised that Shaikh Sultan bin Saif would meet me at Sharjah, and I would either pick up the Duru shaikhs there or at Muscat. In early October we had what we regarded as reliable news that Talib had marched on Salaif and on Ibri and captured both of them. This was followed by a cable to me from Sharjah to say that the Duru shaikhs in some numbers had reached Sharjah, where they clamoured for my presence. As there seemed to be a big party of them, and as there was no need to go to Muscat, where larger planes could not then land, the Company allocated a Dakota in which I flew down to Sharjah where I found all the shaikhs at the BOAC fort. Shaikh Sultan bin Saif was there also.

In those days Sharjah airfield was still very simple and rather rough, much as when I had first seen it six years before. It was still a mud-strip of rolled salt-flat. The fort still did duty for offices, restaurant and sleeping accommodation for any passengers who had to stay the night either on account of bad weather or engine trouble.

I walked across from our Dakota and I saw a large group of bedouin gathered around the door of the fort. From among them, the short square figure of Shaikh Sultan bin Saif, whom I already knew, came forward to greet me. As usual, he was smiling and soon he was laughing as we exchanged greetings, but when I asked him for news of Ibri, I could see from his eyes that his good humour was only a cover; serious business was in front of us, and he was really very troubled. 'Things look bad at the moment, but,' he brightened again, 'it may, God willing, be all for the best. Some of our people were killed at Silaif, but this has greatly angered the Duru, and all their important shaikhs are here now,' and he pointed to the group about twenty yards away. 'We must talk to them at once, and God willing, we will all go down to Duqm today.'

Then he took me up to them and I shook hands with the old paramount, Shaikh Muhammad Said, and his son, Matar; and Shaikh Sultan bin Saif introduced me to Ali bin Hilal, Harib, Musallim and others of the leading shaikhs whom I had not yet met. Even the aged paramount, who was usually calm and totally uninterested in his surroundings, appeared excited. Ali, who I soon found was inclined to be more excitable anyway, was quivering with the intense feeling which his words showed had mastered him. His excitable bedouin talk was not easy to follow as we made our way into the fort. As soon as the usual greetings had been exchanged, starting, I noted with some amusement, with the habitual 'All is quiet in the country; praise be to God,' he began attacking me with, 'When are we going to Ibri?' And the others crowded close to me, taking up the chorus.

As we made our way into the fort and up the stone steps to the roof where there was an awning and which I thought would be the only place where we could sit both in the breeze and under a shade, Ali was pulling at my arm and gesticulating and protesting, behaving as if I had already refused point-blank to go to Ibri. 'Oh followers, oh people; troubles now face us! But, God willing . . .' He turned, and in resonant tones began to address his fellow shaikhs and followers, stressing the urgency of the situation.

He wore the beige cotton shirt, the dark yellow headcloth and thin head-rope often affected by the true nomad; in his hand he had a camel stick (a follower carried his rifle), and at his waist, on a thin belt, was the elaborately carved silver sheath of his Omani dagger. He looked the part of the bedouin chief, thin lips, excited eyes, eloquent in the liquid dialect of the sands. He had a presence when addressing his people, and he plainly carried them with him: that all those who clustered importunately around me shared his excitement was only too clear. Shaikh Sultan bin Saif was amused because he could see I could not get in a word, and he made much ado to get us all seated on the carpets which had been brought up on to the roof for us.

We spent the best part of the day talking under the canvas awning on the roof of the fort, and I was deeply thankful for the presence of Shaikh Sultan bin Saif. The Duru wanted our absolute guarantee that the Sultan of Muscat's forces would drive Talib out of Ibri, Silaif and Tanaam. In their minds they were justifiably confused as to what my position was. They seemed to think that I controlled the army. After all, I evidently had an aeroplane: I could, therefore, do anything. So they insisted I had to promise that I would ensure that Ibri and Tanaam would be recaptured before they would agree to come with me to Duqm. If I did not make this promise in advance, they would go back and make peace with Talib. I tried to explain my position as a Company official and promised to do my best. They were not convinced that I did not actually represent the Sultan of Muscat. It was Shaikh Sultan bin Saif who finally persuaded them to accompany us to Duqm and with no absolute commitment apparently made on either side. By this time, evening was approaching, and the pilot said he had no flying hours left, could not land at Duqm after dark and so on. What with pressure from the pilot (who was quite justified) on one side, and the intransigence of the Duru on the other, it was a trying day; and at the very last there was a hitch, for the pilot would not allow the wild looking Duru on board with their rifles; and the Duru would not get into such an outlandish looking thing as an aeroplane without them. But honour was satisfied when the Duru were persuaded to put some of their ammunition (the pilot thought it was all of it) in the freight locker.

We took off, and our flight path took us right over Ibri which looked peaceful far below us on the desert's edge in the pink light of the setting sun. Well after dark we came into Duqm and landed with the aid of two or three emergency flares on the rough desert strip. As soon as we reached the camp I discussed the position with Angus Perks, Nick Fallon and the geologists, and we agreed that if I could persuade Percy to give us an escort we would make an early start. Angus, who was in overall charge of the Duqm operation, had ready for us all the trucks and supplies we needed. I then went off that night with the leading shaikhs to Nafun to confirm that Percy Coriat would give us an escort, hoping against hope he would be flexible and agree.

It was there that we really came up against it. Coriat said he had specific orders by radio from the Sultan from far-off Dhufar not to go to Ibri, but said he would bend his instructions and go to Fahud if the Duru agreed. Shaikh Sultan bin Saif and I discussed it. He had a simple idea in his mind. 'We [pointing to me] will go to Fahud and argue there,' he said. His intention was to get the Company into the lead and then, if need be, we would all go into Ibri; the army would have to support us. Percy gave orders to that effect to his officers. I was naturally not altogether happy about this, but it seemed the only thing we could do. I felt we must be frank with the Duru shaikhs, of whom Ali bin Hilal had now become the spokesman and effective leader, despite the presence of the old paramount Muhammad bin Said. I told the Duru, therefore, that we could only go and see what was happening; and, although we hoped to be able to get them at least into Tanaam, we could not promise that the army would enter the village. As far as Ibri was concerned, we must wait and see how things developed. The Duru shaikhs, at length, reluctantly agreed to go on these terms. They had no alternative, and I, for my part, had to be content with the thought that no one else could do any better for them. If they made peace with Talib, that might put an end to all exploration for oil. We were their best hope, and they knew it.

We got back to our camp, Duqm, well after midnight. A start in three hours' time at 4 a.m., on the 19 October 1954, was arranged and our aim was to go to Harashif at a point out in the open desert where Angus Perks had earlier arranged a large dump of petrol and water in cans in preparation, and then to press on that same day towards the Wadi al-Amairi, just south of Fahud. The journey would be some two hundred miles and we did not expect to find any water on our way. The geologists thought we might possibly find it in the Wadi al-Amairi; the Duru reported brackish wells in that area, but we had no accurate knowledge of its quantity or potability.

At this critical point and thereafter I was very well supported by Angus Perks, who was senior to me in the Company but, as I was his adviser on concessionary affairs, accepted my word without question as to when and where we could go and supported me completely in all decisions which I made. He had sufficient authority to do this without reference to exploration headquarters in Qatar with whom he was in contact only intermittently by radio and aircraft. The conditions in the summer for radio were poor at Duqm, especially during dust-storms. Angus was a tower of strength and an extremely effective leader in the field under the appalling conditions which the Company's employees had suffered all through that dreadful summer, so often blotted out as they were for days by dust-storms and the tremendous heat, which the tents only increased.

10

Trying Again

The navigation for this trip was done by our surveyor, Nick; the geologists Morton and McGinty were with us and the forty-six soldiers who formed our escort were under the command of Major Michael O'Kelly of the MFF. We had with us the Shaikh of Ibri, Muhammad bin Abdullah al-Yaaqubi; all the Duru shaikhs and some followers; and of course Shaikh Sultan bin Saif. As water and food were so important we took virtually no camp kit, only a roll of blankets each and the most elementary cooking equipment; this was how we were to live for several weeks. The Duru gave me a good deal of trouble since each follower insisted on sitting like their shaikhs in the front seat of a lorry or Land Rover, and there were not enough front seats to go round. These men, who had travelled hitherto only on camels, felt, justifiably in the circumstances, that it was beneath their dignity to ride on the back of a lorry with the troops. However, after much talk I sorted the problem out and we set off.

To begin with the going was good and after Harashif, where we were refuelled from the drums we had dumped, we came to a piece of open desert the like of which I have never seen before or since. It was perfectly flat and extended some seventy miles. The surface was of light sand on a gravel base, and there was not a sign of an animal or an insect or a plant upon it: the surface was smooth and flat without a mark. It seemed a shame to sully its smoothness, as we cruised over it at fifty miles an hour. The bedouin said they had never crossed it, as it lay well off all their routes, and I doubted whether any living thing had crossed it before. On the other side, we came into rough country where the winter rain water from the distant mountains ran across the broad gravel plain and then into and under the sands. Far as we were from the mountains, this produced a maze of winding, narrow, dried-up water-courses; no sooner had you crossed one than you were in another. It always looked as if some other route would be easier, but if you tried it, the alternative usually turned out worse. These twists and turns delayed us and made navigation more difficult. Nick, our surveyor, was a first-class desert navigator, and each night he could fix our position exactly by stellar observation with a theodolite.

We had counted on reaching the Wadi al-Amairi on the second night and visiting Fahud on the third day, but by dusk on 20 October we were only in the Wadi Musallim and there we stayed the night. The Duru were fascinated by the route which we had taken. They had expected us to take a long circuitous trail partly through the sands of the eastern edge of the Empty Quarter where there were a few brackish wells. Since we were self-sufficient as far as water was concerned, we had taken an absolutely direct route, only veering off a straight compass line when we had to avoid particularly bad going. We had already formed some idea of the country from aerial reconnaissance, and the route which we were able to choose in consequence was unknown even to the best travelled of the Duru. When we got into the area of the *wadis* we were in country that was familiar to them, and the Duru could help us in establishing names of *wadis* and dunes and could advise us on the positions of water holes.

We set off early on 21 October after morning tea and biscuits. The Duru were finding our food very trying. Out of politeness, they wanted to eat with us, but they preferred the soldiers' food and at mealtimes would dodge from one group to the other. I remember one of the Duru being given an open tin of sardines. He smelt it and tipped it disgustedly on to the sand. He preferred his fish 'fresh', although theirs was often old, and dried in the sun on the sand; tinned fish was unnatural they thought. We did no cooking and, beyond making tea and Nescafé and heating up soup, we lived on cold tinned food and biscuits. The troops boiled rice every night, and, of course, the Duru thought this much more civilized than having to rough it on sardines and tinned salmon.

As we approached the Amairi, Musallim, one of the head shaikhs of the Duru, said he expected to find some of his men there, and he wanted to warn them in advance that a large party with Europeans and troops was coming with the agreement of their tribal leaders. Otherwise, scared tribesmen would, he thought, loose off their rifles at us. This seemed sensible, so I drove on ahead with Musallim and one of his colleagues, and they guided me successfully down into the *wadi* bed, rough gravel about twenty feet below the level of the plain, and to the well Muqbarah, an unlined, shallow water hole where there were several trees, thick bushes and clumps of grass. We got down from my Land Rover and slung a bucket down the well to try the water which proved sweet.

I heard a movement in the bushes and Musallim shouted, giving his name and asking who the person in hiding was. A very scared looking tribesman eventually emerged, clutching his rifle by the barrel. He said he had been with a party of Duru at the well overnight. Early in the morning they had heard the sound of our engines and at first thought it was the noise of airliners which commonly fly over at a great height. But it soon became evident to them that this was something different, and at last they could see the tall plumes of dust which our trucks were throwing up. All his companions went off on their camels to warn other Duru camping further up the *wadi* to get their families out of the way and to concert some way of attacking the intruders; he had been left behind to hide and to spy upon these strange invaders. To him we might have been creatures from Mars. This was the first time that anyone had come to the Amairi on anything but a camel, and many of the Duru had never seen a car.

Musallim told him who we all were and sent him off on his camel to explain to his fellow tribesmen that there was nothing to fear. His camel was about a quarter of a mile away among the trees, hobbled with a rope between the front legs in the customary way, and he went to fetch it. Musallim told me that he wanted to meet as many of his people as he could and to send them up and down the more populated parts of the Wadi al-Amairi and Wadi al-Aswad to warn other tribesmen of what was going on and to explain that we were there with the agreement of their tribal leaders. As all the ranging grounds of the Duru are totally exclusive to the one tribe, they will let no one in without permission and they seldom give such permission.

We could now see clearly that the area was a dangerous one for bedouin of other tribes. Water holes were very few, and round most of them would be Duru camping. It was impossible for a party on camels to cross the area without the knowledge and agreement of the Duru. The same can be said of the tribal area of the Al Bu Shams to the north; but Duru country is so much more extensive that no one could possibly travel over these vast wastes by camel without the agreement of the tribe. Our cars, however, had introduced a new dimension to desert travel in this area, and only in cars could such a sudden incursion as ours have been made.

This total exclusivity of desert ranges may be unusual in Arabia, for although in other parts with which I am familiar tribal ranges are recognized as belonging mainly to particular tribes, arrangements can be made for other tribes to cross them or to spend a whole season grazing over them. In the case of the Duru their lands lead nowhere and there is no point in any other tribe crossing them. The tribes of the hills do not venture far into the desert. The tribes to the north and south of the Duru travel mainly towards the north-east to the settled villages of Oman, and over to the west of the Duru's area lies the Empty Quarter. The Duru themselves cross their own territory in search of grazing for their camels, they dig salt from large salt deposits in the desert, and they make and carry charcoal. At the season of the ripening of their dates, they take their families to the plantations in the settled foothills, but they tend to camp away from the larger towns. This is partly because of the strong instinct of the bedouin to stay out in the desert as long as possible; they can never be happy for long in settled areas. There is some evidence for thinking that one of their reasons for disliking staying even one night in or near Ibri is a fear of malaria which they told me they attribute to devils which inhabit date trees in the gardens. This is not an unreasonable assumption; there has been bad malarial infection in many parts of Oman, and there can be no mosquitoes except when there is irrigation or open water wells.

Musallim advised us to camp at Muqbarah and the other shaikhs agreed. It would give the bedouin time to hear about us. Evidently the noise of our coming, especially that of the big six-wheeler Nubian trucks in which we carried the soldiers, would precede us for up to three hours, in those totally silent wastes, depending on the wind and, of course, our speed. In the difficult and the slower going of the *wadis*, we might be announcing ourselves many hours ahead. The halt at Muqbarah enabled us to put all our vehicles in order. On the previous night we had to send our motor mechanic back to Duqm since he had suffered severe burns in an accident with a Primus stove. He was driven back non-stop by one of our best drivers and taken to Qatar by air where, after a long stay in hospital, he recovered completely. The vehicles were suffering mostly from choked filters and suspension breakages, and the half-day in the *wadi* enabled these faults to be put right.

We went up a small hill near the camp and could see to the north the outline of Jabal Fahud and to the north-east and east the far-off mountains of Oman in which Talib and his army were sitting. What were they doing we wondered. I could not help thinking how Thesiger must have felt camping near here with his party of only four or five bedouin, reliant solely on his wits and the loyalty of his companions. We found that the water was plentiful and drinkable, and this was a very great help since it meant that we need not send vehicles back to Duqm for water. Our main worry from now on would be the fuel for the vehicles, but we carried sufficient for the next two days. On 23 October, we expected a larger party to come up with Angus Perks, Colonel Percy Coriat, some more troops and several loads of petrol. We had a radio with us and could speak to Duqm and, as soon as we had tried the water at Muqbarah, we sent a message asking for an alteration in the loading of the next convoy. From now on, our need would be for petrol, not water, and also for empty barrels in order to exploit the water supply in the Amairi, and any other sources we might find.

As we ate our evening meal by the well in the Wadi al-Amairi and discussed the future of the expedition, we felt rather more cheerful. But on the political side I had fresh cause for misgivings. During the late afternoon several tribesmen had come in to see Musallim and the other shaikhs. They told us that several people had been killed in the first attack on Silaif by Talib's men, that Ibri had fallen with very little fighting, and that Talib had left a strong garrison in Ibri fort under a leader called Safyan. Some said that Tanaam, the seat of the principal Duru shaikhs, had fallen to Talib and some said it had not.

The Duru shaikhs had now become highly excited again and insisted that we should immediately go to Tanaam with the troops to recapture it if necessary. With great difficulty I managed to persuade them that we must await the arrival of the Colonel with the main body of men. They reluctantly agreed to stay one more day in the Amairi. Next day they sent only one sleepy tribesman with us when we set off as a small party with the geologists and Nick to look at Fahud, take rock samples to assess its age, and look for and mark out an airstrip. Our little party successfully accomplished all our tasks during the morning, and we had lunch amongst the rocks of Fahud.

It was exciting to have reached Fahud at last; although the scene was inevitably what we expected. This was because we had all flown over it so many times and had photographed Fahud from the air, that it did not

Sharjah airstrip, 1948. This point is now near the middle of downtown Sharjah   (*R. Codrai*)

Drilling at Jabal Ali, Dubai. Shaikh Said bin Maktum with the author   (*R.Codrai*)

Jabal Fahud from the air, 1950   (*R.Codrai*)

Murani fort, Muscat (R. Codrai)

Shaikh Sultan bin Saif al-Hawsini in 1988   (*Rehma Studio al-Khabura*)

His Highness Shaikh Shakhbut welcomes His Highness the Sultan of Muscat to
al-Ain in December 1955

Colonel Eric Johnson meets people in Buraimi after the fighting has stopped

Silaif, Oman   (*R. Codrai*)

Abu Dhabi fort with the British Agency in the foreground, 1956   (*R.Codrai*)

leave anything much new to see. Whenever geologists were on board the aircraft, we used to circle slowly around it at a few hundred feet to get a closer look, and very uncomfortable this was on a hot bumpy day. From the air we had seen the cirque formed by the harder strata which remained when the softer ones, particularly those near the middle, were gradually weathered over millions of years. These harder strata have, in turn, been cut off leaving the springing of the arch as ridges sticking out of the plain, the whole of the upper part of the dome being removed by weathering. As you approach it across the desert, Fahud looks like any other mountain of brown limestone in the desert. If you drive into the cirque, the nature of the formation is apparent and you can see where the strata have been broken off or worn away to leave those ridges which are all that remain above the surface of what once must have been a whaleback mountain.

In the desert below the rocks on one side there was some shrub and some of those very unpleasant plants (*harm* and *arad* in Arabic) which grow in salty water. The bedouin warned us not to dig for water in this area. It was too salty, and this we later found was the case. We would have to rely on wells in the Wadi al-Amairi. The geologists were hopeful that later, by drilling deeper wells, we would probably find water. So at last we were in Fahud, but would we ever get the chance to drill? Could we maintain ourselves here? The sleepy Duru guide we had with us, like all his fellows, was obviously agreeable to anything but only if we went to Ibri, the little town nestling in the pale blue mountains on our horizon. It was in Ibri that we should find the answer.

When we returned to camp we found that Angus Perks, Percy Coriat and the main party of troops had arrived from Duqm. Our little camp in the *wadi* bed looked larger and busier when we got back to it. The shaikhs had grouped themselves under trees by the well. The troops were established on vantage points above us on the edge of the main plateau fifty yards or so from the water, and the oil company party had grouped itself a little down the *wadi*. Still we had no tents, but there was now an adequate number of empty drums for water, there were piles of petrol drums, and a small pump was chugging away by the well. Angus Perks had brought bad news: he said that after we had left, Coriat, who had come up with him, had received direct orders by radio at Nafun from the Sultan not to take the troops into either Tanaam or Ibri. If this was so it looked as if the whole basis of agreement with the Duru had been cut away, and I explained to Angus the falseness of our position as it would now seem to the shaikhs; unless we took them at least into Tanaam we should be breaking our word. My assessment of the conflicting evidence available was that the Imam had probably not taken Tanaam, since we knew the village had no proper fort; and as it could not therefore be easily defended by a garrison of Talib's men against the Duru, we thought it would not have been worth their while to capture it, and thus risk a counter-attack in which they would be outnumbered.

The aged Shaikh Muhammed, his son Matar, and Shaikhs Ali bin Hilal and Musallim on every occasion I met them in the camp were all pestering me to get them into Tanaam; and I suggested to Angus that if we could take the shaikhs into Tanaam in Company transport, the MFF could remain some distance short of it. The effect in Ibri would be much the same as if troops had actually reached Tanaam; and at that point we should have to think up some way of getting the Imam's men out of Ibri. Angus and I went over to Percy Coriat. We found him gloomy. He now had, he said, altogether ninety-six troops with him. They were too young and inexperienced and all ill-trained. Many had been in the force only as long as a month, and hardly knew how to fire their rifles, let alone move into an attack as a cohesive body. Apart from rifles he had only a few Brens and two-inch mortars; and neither weapon is suitable for an attack on a solid fort. He repeated that he had direct orders not to enter Tanaam. Angus then asked him innocently, 'But do you not have an overriding order to protect the Company in all circumstances?' 'Of course, this is what we are here for.' 'Well, then, the shaikhs insist on our taking them into Tanaam. We shall have to drive them there. All we ask you to do is to come up close enough to be in support if we get into trouble.'

The argument went on and on around these points. We were sitting on the sand under a tree near the Company area. In the middle of this discussion one of the Duru came over and said to me, ' The shaikh wants you.' I said, 'I'll be over in a minute.' 'What,' I said to Percy Coriat, 'am I to say to them? They will be insisting on our going to Tanaam at once.' 'You must not say that I will take the troops into Tanaam or Ibri. Anything else you say about the Company is your own business, but you must not make any promise about the troops.' He spoke quite angrily. It was plain how much his orders had upset him, and how much he wanted to help us.

After further discussion with Angus, who was prepared to support me in any move which seemed essential, I decided to tell the shaikhs quite plainly that the Company party would go on to Tanaam taking the Duru with us, within the next three days. The troops would, we hoped, be close to us, but more than that I could not promise. As I expected they simply replied, 'What if the Imam's men are in Tanaam already? What of the threat to burn our trees in Tanaam and Ibri? These trees are the wealth of our tribe. Whoever has our trees has a knife at our throats.' The discussion went on until midnight, and it was finally agreed that on the following morning, 24 October, Angus Perks and Nick Fallon would take some of the shaikhs up nearer Tanaam, reconnoitre the route, dump petrol, seek intelligence and return to camp at Muqbarah. On the 26th at the latest, if it proved practical, we would go with the shaikhs into Tanaam.

Ali then asked me for money to help him to collect some followers to make us look more impressive. I tried to argue that in this crisis surely we did not need to pay his men. Ali said he knew his men; they would have to abandon their families, wherever they might be, to join him; and an inducement was needed to get them to do this immediately. I had two tin trunks full of silver Maria Theresa dollars, the most acceptable currency of the interior at that time; and I agreed to pay one Maria Theresa dollar a day to each man who stayed with Ali for as long as the crisis lasted. These solid silver copies of the eighteenth-century coin were still accepted in the interior of Oman.

The following morning, Angus and Nick and a few of the shaikhs went off to the Wadi Aswad without any troops, but with some Duru, while the geologists visited Fahud again on their own. The geologists were now confident from their first look at the fossils that the rock was of the right age and this, therefore, made the oil prospects good in the Fahud structure. Only drilling, however, could now give us the final answer; but this raised all our hopes and made me all the more desperately keen to overcome what looked insuperable political obstacles. To be baulked now would be hard indeed. The shaikhs left me in peace all that day. It was hot and dusty in camp, but the air was dry and by evening the desert became pleasantly cool. I spent some of the day making notes on water wells and interrogating the tribesmen who came to see us on this important topic. I also recruited some more tribesmen with the Maria Theresa dollars.

Nick and Angus returned before dusk to report comparatively good going, and that a good well lay on our route called Tawi Murri. The shaikhs had got hold of several followers in the Wadi Aswad whom we would pick up when we went forward. My main trouble now was with the Company drivers who drove the big Nubians, and who said not unreasonably that they were not soldiers and they had heard there might be fighting. We had no drivers for our Land Rovers, and drove these ourselves to save carrying more men and consequently more food and water than necessary, but the big vehicles with the troops and petrol were essential, and there were not enough of us to drive them ourselves. None of the soldiers could drive except the three British officers, who like us, had a Land Rover each. I was, therefore, forced to agree to paying double overtime to keep the drivers with us, and on this basis they served us loyally for the rest of the expedition. News as regards Tanaam was still conflicting, but we had cheering intelligence that the Ibri garrison was small and that the Imam and his brother had gone to Rustaq with his army.

A convoy of vehicles had meanwhile gone back to Duqm and returned with a few more troops and more fuel. Percy Coriat now had one hundred and twenty-six men in all. He said his own ill-prepared, tiny force, although safe enough in vehicles in the desert, would be vulnerable to a mass attack by tribesmen when in the close country of the foothills at Ibri. I thought this appreciation was only too realistic. On 25 October we set off in six Land Rovers and five Nubians, taking all the MFF party except a small guard for Muqbarah camp, all the shaikhs and their followers and, from the Company, Angus, Nick, the five drivers and myself. We had an easy trip up to the Aswad, and camped there for the night. We gave Shaikh Ali a driver and a vehicle to help him round up followers, and a dozen or so were collected and joined him that evening, when I held my first pay parade for the tribesmen.

Percy Coriat, Angus and I then drew up a simple plan for the next day. The three Company Land Rovers driven by Angus, Nick and myself would take the shaikhs into Tanaam, followed by a Nubian with the tribesmen. Percy would halt a mile or two short of Tanaam and we would send word back. If we were in trouble he would come up and help us, if we were not he would camp not far away. The shaikhs thought it a crazy plan to have the troops behind us, but somehow we got them to agree to it. I did not emphasize very precisely what the MFF would or would not do, I said the military are a law unto themselves, but I trusted them to protect us in whatever way they saw fit. Fortunately at no time did the shaikhs attempt to talk to Percy Coriat. Had they heard directly from him quite how closely he had been restricted by his orders, I do not believe they would have gone on with this operation.

On the following morning our little column of vehicles set off for Tanaam. It was not very far, and the going was good. Nick was in the lead, followed by Angus, myself with the shaikhs and one Nubian with the tribesmen in it. Just before noon, coming over a rise, we saw a village with palm trees: the first sign of permanent habitation we had seen since we had left Duqm nearly a week ago. Behind the village we could see the grey and brown of the hills that surrounded Ibri on its north and, behind them, the blue of the main range of the mountains of Oman, which had been always on our horizon over the last few days. Now they were nearer and looked to me more threatening. The village lay in front of us, peaceful and quiet, the only sounds the noise of the poultry and the creak of a well pulley, a dog barking, the usual village noises. The village consisted of a few mud houses on the edge of a palm grove, and scattered around the houses were many small huts of palm fronds. Smoke was gently rising from fires near the huts and among the houses. The shaikhs said that they thought all must be well in the village, but they were not sure. They had a discussion: 'Drive on,' they said, 'but go slowly as it may be necessary to stop and go in finally on foot.'

We drove on, in my case, at any rate, with some apprehension. We could see people coming out of their huts and gathering. The shaikhs stood up on the seats, hanging on to the windscreens, shouting and waving. As we got closer we saw that everyone was friendly and there was no sign of an enemy. We pulled up and the shaikhs jumped down and were soon surrounded by their people. Shaikh Sultan bin Saif was sitting with me. 'For goodness sake please find out what is going on,' I said to him. 'That may not be too easy to do quickly.' He smiled and disappeared into a noisy group of tribesmen.

Angus and Nick lit cigarettes and we waited as patiently as we could. After some fifteen minutes Shaikh Sultan came back to us and said: 'Talib never came to Tanaam. There was a fight at Silaif and then Ibri fell. He stayed a few days and, leaving a garrison, went back to Nizwa. He returned only a week ago with some men, but then went off to Rustaq. I cannot be sure how big the garrison is, but they are all in the fort in Ibri and do not go out much except in strong force, for fear of the townspeople; but remember Ibri fort is strong and hard to capture.' Meanwhile the big Nubian trucks had come up with more Duru, and with them Shaikh Ali bin Hilal and Matar. When they joined us I suggested that we should bring up more vehicles and camp by the village. Ali wanted the troops to come up as well, and he formally invited them to stay near the village where there was plentiful water.

We sent off the truck to bring up more vehicles and I went to look for Percy Coriat. He was in fact only about half a mile behind us and had been anxiously watching us through binoculars, ready to come in quickly at the first sound of shooting. He laughed when I gave him the Shaikh's invitation and said: 'I think I have nothing to lose now. I shouldn't be here anyway.'

We drove back to Tanaam together and ate our lunch sitting in the cars. It was by now very hot. The Duru told us they had prepared a big meal for the evening and after it they wanted a discussion.

Meanwhile Shaikh Sultan bin Saif had been busy. He said he had found out more about the Ibri garrison. He thought it was not so large and its morale was poor as the townspeople were obstructing them in every way. Muhammad bin Abdullah, the Shaikh of Ibri, who was with our party, had already sent in to his people and ordered as many of his followers as possible to come out to Tanaam to meet him and join with him in an assault on the garrison. Ali bin Hilal and Matar were collecting followers as fast as they could. If they could collect several hundred, we hoped that the Ibri garrison might feel that they could surrender without losing face. If it came to a fight I did not think we could dislodge the garrison: it would have to be done by bluff if it were to be done at all. If we could not dislodge them within a day or two Talib would be back in Ibri with reinforcements and an opportunity would be lost forever.

I went over to Percy Coriat and told him all this. He seemed a new man. Four Land Rovers were standing together in line and troops were climbing into them with Brens, rifles and the tiny two-inch mortars. 'We are off to look at Ibri,' he said with a laugh, waved his stick, jumped into the leading car and away they went. Needless to say the shaikhs were overjoyed when they saw Percy Coriat drive off and heard where he had gone, but unfortunately they assumed that he had simply gone off to capture Ibri, and that nothing further would be required of them. I tried to explain what the army mean by the term 'reconnaissance'.

We knew the topographical features of Ibri and its surroundings from
air photography and from our own recent observation from aircraft. The
town itself nestles right against the foot of a ridge which overlooks it from
the north and east. In the centre the ridge is broken, and a narrow gorge
takes the main bed of the Wadi al-Kabir through it. The cliff on the
westerly edge of this gorge directly overlooks the fort which is embedded
among the houses of the town and has virtually no field of fire. To the
south of the town are the extensive date groves and gardens. The *wadi*
winds past the date gardens and some seven miles away on its edge lies
the village of Tanaam. There is another similar break in the ridge four
miles east of Ibri and here is the well-sited fort on one side of a gorge,
called Silaif. This had been captured by Talib, and then for some reason,
presumably lack of men, had been left without any garrison. Some four
or five miles to the north of Ibri lies the big fortress of Ainain which sits
astride important irrigation channels of the upper *wadi*. This was held by
the Shaikh of Dariz who had accepted the authority of the new Imam
under duress; but the shaikh was reported to be out of sympathy with the
Imam and to favour the Sultan.

It was becoming apparent how much the people of the whole area
disliked Imam Ghalib and his brother Talib; and they evidently were
prepared to throw in their lot with the Sultan's government and hoped
for oil and its riches as a consequence. Talib and Ghalib seemed to them
to have nothing to offer: no administration, no money and no expertise in
regard to oil. Talib's moves about the country with armies were
unpopular as the villagers had to feed the troops.

The Sultan of Muscat was faced with the difficulty that he had no
source of revenue sufficient to enable him to develop and administer the
interior. At the moment when he succeeded his father in 1931 the state
treasury was in debt. By the early 1950s the books balanced, but he had a
large domain. The coastline of Oman is over one thousand miles in
length; the population of Oman was then believed to be about seven
hundred and fifty thousand, but it may have been a million. There were
no roads, no developed water system, there was only one small
missionary hospital in the whole country and there was no electricity
outside the capital, very little in it. The highest mountains reach to ten
thousand feet. The villages were in separate valleys making communication both between them and the coast and between each other

difficult; even if revenues were available, development of such an area, with difficult climatic conditions, was a daunting challenge. The Sultan kept assuring us he was desperately anxious to find the revenue through the oil in order to develop the country. The oil, if it existed, was almost certain to be found under the desert, in the Duru's ranging grounds, but the mountainous interior stood between the coast and any potential oilfield. He needed to extend his authority and to replace tribal influence with direct rule.

Under the Agreement of Sib in theory some arrangement might have been made to develop the oil resources by agreement with the tribes, but I had had little hope in that direction. Now Talib had broken the traditional observation of the Sib Agreement by seizing Ibri, and if only he could be driven out again by the MFF, it seemed that the way might be open for the Sultan to establish direct rule, at least in the oilfield area to give time to the Company to prospect and produce. If Talib were allowed to continue his attempt to make a separate country out of the interior, against the wish as we knew of many of the tribes, no stability could be secured in which any oil company could work. Progress would be postponed indefinitely. The key to the whole problem lay in the establishment of the authority of the Sultan in Ibri, and its extension over the whole of the interior.

Late in the afternoon Percy Coriat came back, looking excited and pleased. He explained that he had put patrols for a short time up on the heights to the north and east of Ibri. There had been a little shooting from the town, but none of it effectively directed, and some might even have been in greeting. He proposed repeating his patrol with nearly all his men early on the following morning; and he suggested that this would give an opportunity for the shaikhs to put men into the groves to the south, and the fort would be surrounded at least in appearance.

He calculated that although militarily such an operation made no sense at all, yet in view of the low morale of the garrison and their ignorance of the real weakness of the MFF detachment, success might come of it. Not only was morale of the garrison reported to be low, their supplies and ammunition were said to be insufficient and their numbers apparently somewhere between fifty and two hundred. The townspeople were obstructing them, and they hardly dared to go out of the fort except in large parties and armed. He said if only the Company would produce an aircraft to do a demonstration run low over the town this should do the trick on its own.

I discussed all this with Angus. He would like to ask for an aircraft to fly a demonstration, but he did not think the Company would agree; however he agreed it made sense to put the troops and the tribesmen in position round the fort and see what came of it. Nick had marked out a strip for use in an emergency near Tanaam, and we could land a Dove or Dakota there to evacuate any casualties. We had to be content with that. The whole operation hinged on persuading the shaikhs to co-operate, and after a hasty evening meal of rice and sheep with the Duru under their trees, I asked the leading shaikhs to draw aside for talks. First I had a long talk with Shaikh Sultan bin Saif, to which Ali bin Hilal listened. I explained what Percy Coriat had planned for the morning. Sultan concurred with Percy's view and said that if we could get several hundred men into the lower town, and at the same time dominate the fort, or appear to do so, with troops on the heights, and move our vehicles about ostentatiously on the open ground between the *wadi* and the hill to the east, where they could be seen from the fort, there was a very good chance that things would go as we wished. His information about the feeling in the surrounding area was that Dariz would accept the Sultan, Silaif could be easily garrisoned, as its fort was empty, and only the Baluch in al-Araqi looked like giving us any trouble once Ibri fort had fallen.

Encouraged by this advice I went with him across to where the main group of Duru Shaikhs were sitting under the trees. We did not have much difficulty in persuading them to agree to the sort of action we had in mind. My only problem was that the need to give each irregular one Maria Theresa dollar a day would soon exhaust my stock of cash, and I had no means of getting more until we had established an air supply route. I made it a rule that I would only pay those who had left their families in the desert to join us; from now on people from the immediate area would have to join for the sake of the cause. Muhammad bin Abdullah al-Yaaqubi, shaikh of the settled people of Ibri, made strong objections, and said that, if any money was being given, his people would need some of it. So I said, right, no money for anyone.

Considerable wrangling ensued as a result of this remark of mine, but in the end it was agreed that if Muhammad could have some of his people taken up by truck that night, they would assemble as many armed men as possible in the date groves by first light, and no money would be needed for them. All the Duru would be sent to join them in the Nubians: the Duru now numbered some three hundred, of whom I was paying some one hundred and fifty or so. The trucks would then return to pick up the main body of troops, the advance guard going up with the Colonel just before first light to make sure of taking the commanding positions on the heights.

It does not take long to put that on paper, but it took almost all night to arrange. I went back and concerted these plans with Percy Coriat and Angus Perks and I felt that everything possible had been covered. We had little time for sleeping, and before dawn we saw Percy's column move off, the bedouin having already been put in position during the night under the charge of Shaikh Musallim and some of his younger colleagues. Shaikh Muhammad bin Abdullah had taken his party into the town, where he meant to raise all the able-bodied men he could. He was also intending to ensure that messages from different sources would reach the garrison to the effect that a large force had arrived, of which we were only the advance party; tanks were on their way; all the Duru had gathered in the groves and numbered many hundreds; and all the townspeople had taken up arms to eject the garrison.

Nick, Angus and I were busy in the first hours of the operation supervising the transport and, at about seven o'clock when the Nubians had been loaded and dispatched with the last batch of troops, we went up ourselves to see what was going on.

11

The End of the Beginning

Although it was still early, the sun was well up as we drove into the narrow gravel plain made by the junction of the Wadi al-Kabir and the Wadi al-Ain. These flat gravel beds are typical of this part of Oman and like the deeper *wadis* out in the desert are made by the flash floods in the mountains, running across the plain to disappear eventually under the sands of the Empty Quarter. Close in to the foothills as we were, the *wadi* bed is wide and level and, although bumpy enough, comparatively easy going for a Land Rover or truck and much better than the narrow channels we had encountered further south. There are ridges of larger rocks, but for the most part the gravel is even in texture. Over to our left was sandy scrub country with acacia and other desert trees, a few of the straggley, gaunt, tall *bu Samra* among them. Half a mile to our right was the same sort of country, with now the first foothills closing in on us. We passed a ruined village and fort, light brown mud walls matching the soil, with a few bedraggled palm trees and the remains of a garden, which Sultan told us was Dubayshi.

Soon, in the line of the ridge to the east, we could see the break immediately beyond and above Silaif, although the village itself could not be seen for the bushy country between us was slightly raised. This was where some of the recent fighting had been; we were now in the critical area. Leaving the Wadi al-Ain we swung slightly leftwards making towards the point where the foothills rose up beyond Ibri to its north, and immediately in front of us we could see the second break in the ridge which must, we knew, be immediately above Ibri. Some ten minutes later, turning a corner of the *wadi* bed and following the Nubians, we saw the first trees of the Ibri palm groves which stretched southwards from the town for nearly a mile by the side of the *wadi* bed. The steep bare foothills were now closing in to our right and we could see

[131]

in what an interesting, strategic position Ibri lay, overlooked as it was by steep bluffs on two sides.

We could hear no sound of shooting but we thought it wise to climb up out of the gravel *wadi* bed on the eastern side, as the Nubians evidently had done, leaving the date groves to our left and slightly below us. The ridge of Jabal Kawas was only half a mile to our right, and beyond the palm trees on the left of the *wadi* we could now see the pale brown of the mud buildings and the larger turrets of the fortress among the houses. After crossing so many miles of desert it was moving to see this township among the groves, nestling under the bare brown and pink hillside, sprawling, silent, seemingly deserted in the warm morning air; but on this particular morning our knowledge that some three hundred armed men were in the groves and Percy Coriat's men of the MFF were even now in position somewhere on the crags to the north and east above us, while a potential enemy sat silently in the main fort, added excitement to the scene. We were again following the tracks of the Nubians and now we could see them and a few Land Rovers drawn up on the right of the *wadi*, close under the foothills, and perhaps three hundred yards from the edge of the date gardens to our left.

Percy had established himself on the edge of the *wadi* to the east of the town, and his troops were in position on the heights above him. So far, he said, only one shot had been fired from the town. The town was strangely still, but people were now to be seen coming out of the edge of the town into the groves, and the Duru were walking through the trees towards fort and town. Unfortunately only those near the edge of the grove or in the *wadi* were visible, and we were not certain that the garrison in the fort could see even these, as trees tended to screen them.

We established ourselves on a small hillock near Percy's headquarters. Shaikh Sultən bin Saif was still with us, but by now we had lost touch with most of the shaikhs, who were I hoped fulfilling their part of the operation by encouraging the tribesmen in the town and groves. Nothing seemed to be happening near the fort and as time went on it began to look as if nothing would happen.

I suggested to Shaikh Sultan that we should get hold of a reliable emissary in order to take an ultimatum to the garrison. Percy Coriat at once said he would not have anything to do with this; but Sultan bin Saif agreed and Nick Fallon drove him to the edge of the town and was to go back and pick him up later. About an hour afterwards he appeared with two men and Nick went down and fetched them. The two men with him were prominent citizens of the town, well known and respected.

Shaikh Sultan bin Saif then wrote a note as the representative of the Sultan of Muscat. We both realized that the Sultan would never approve of such a note, and if we failed Shaikh Sultan would be in trouble, so would I. If we succeeded perhaps we should be forgiven. In it the commander of the garrison, who we had learned was named Saifyan, was offered a safe-conduct to come and talk to Shaikh Sultan with a view to agreeing terms of surrender and to saving the lives of the garrison. The military position was described in the note and the numbers of those with arms, who were gathered to attack, was given. The two men were taken to the edge of the town and disappeared into its streets carrying the message.

It was now eleven in the morning of a very hot autumn day. The place we had chosen had no shade, but we felt we should not move, since the letter had described where Shaikh Sultan would receive Saifyan, and we were in clear view from the fort whose garrison, as we intended, could see all that was going on around us, with troops and vehicles moving ostentatiously. Angus organized several of the big Nubians to make runs from behind one small hill to behind another and then come back by a roundabout route and repeat the process. The dust and the noise they made was considerable and gave the impression of a large fleet of vehicles to the watchers in the fort. We waited an hour and I was losing patience and hope, when our two Ibri citizens reappeared at the edge of the town; two other men were with them. Nick Fallon went across to pick them up. As they came towards us Shaikh Sultan told me that he was sure one of the two men was Saifyan himself, and this proved to be the case. The second man was a follower.

Saifyan stepped slowly down from the Land Rover and walked over to where we were standing. He was a short, rather insignificant looking man, in a dark cloak with a white turban. As was only to be expected he looked unhappy and uneasy when Shaikh Sultan, whom he recognized at once, introduced him to me. Then he took Saifyan aside and sat down with him. After about half an hour's talk, by which time we were in an agony of suspense and curiosity, Shaikh Sultan came over and said, 'It's no good, he says we must all go away, we have no right here, and if we do not go Talib will come and destroy us.' Percy Coriat, who had joined us, fumed when he heard this. 'Tell the silly idiot we have surrounded him, show him the troops and the Duru down in the grove.' (Many of the latter were now plainly visible from where we were). 'I have done that,' said Shaikh Sultan. Percy looked angry and he went over and spoke to Saifyan in Arabic; his determination to keep out of politics seemed suddenly to have evaporated. He said that he guaranteed to let them go safely out of the area and back to Nizwa if they surrendered, otherwise the fort would be attacked and some might be killed. He left us snorting indignantly and went back to his troops. I then tried my hand, and afterwards asked Shaikh Sultan to have another go. I thought perhaps that things might swing our way. Percy had evidently made an impression. At length, after what seemed a long time, Shaikh Sultan came over to us and said that Saifyan had agreed to instruct his men to surrender. A note was to be taken to the fort by the follower, with the instruction that the men should come out.

We were, however, not altogether sure if all was well and I, therefore, suggested to Shaikh Sultan that it would be wise to have the note intercepted. This was done and we were not so very surprised to find that it said something very different. It told Saifyan's men that he was being held prisoner and they must not surrender. Percy was back with us again when we learnt this interesting development, and he managed to look very fierce and angry and said something very loudly to Sultan bin Saif about the danger of double-crossing him. Saifyan seemed to take note of this and looked unhappy.

By now it was nearly three in the afternoon and we had all been sitting in the hot sun, occasionally refreshed by coffee produced by one of the Yaaqib. I thought that our physical discomfort could only help us, as Saifyan seemed to suffer the heat worse than we did. I said to Shaikh Sultan, 'Please tell him again that we know he must agree to the surrender proposal, he and his men will be safe, better for all of us that he should make his mind up quickly.' Shaikh Sultan had another long talk and this ended with Saifyan writing a letter which ordered the garrison to come out and meet us at the edge of the town. This was dispatched by hand of the follower.

There was another long wait during which I think we all had made up our minds that there was another trick being played. None of us had slept much, if at all, the night before, or indeed for several nights, we were all extremely tired, and we realized that if the garrison did not come out there was nothing that we could do to force them to do so. An ignominious rebuff seemed only too likely, and we knew what His

Highness the Sultan in Salalah would say if we failed. Only Angus remained cheerful and optimistic. I myself once more felt that the thing was going wrong.

Suddenly Nick shouted, 'I think they are coming.' A rather sad collection of fifty men, some young, some rather elderly, all in traditional Omani headgear and Arab robes and cloaks, were filing past the corner house of the town into the open in front of us. Percy looked most relieved, but said it was up to Shaikh Sultan bin Saif to take the surrender; he would stay where he was, he had no permission to take part in this sort of thing. I suggested to Shaikh Sultan that they should lay down their arms. These would be put in one of our trucks, and with Saifyan and a follower, they would be taken a short way up the track towards Nizwa and deposited under a tree. The garrison could walk there and pick them up. Food and water would be provided to start them off, but they must make their own way out of the area. Shaikh Sultan agreed, and we went across to speak to them.

It was a scene I shall never forget. The fifty men had walked slowly out of the gap between the houses which gave on to the *wadi* bed where we now were. They made a line in the shade with their backs to a wall which enlcosed a date grove. As I have said earlier, the Omani is a proud man, he walks with short quick steps holding his body stiffly upright, head back, and with a natural grace. Their very way of walking distinguishes them. These men were all Omanis, their jaunty spriteliness had gone, but yet they held their customary pose with dignity. Not surprisingly they seemed astonished. They had never seen foreigners, certainly not Europeans, before. They were surrendering to Shaikh Sultan and to an Arab force, yet who were these strange people with them, what were these huge vehicles that had brought them? These were the first strangers to come from the south, the first vehicles of their kind to come to Ibri from anywhere. No wonder they looked amazed.

I felt that I ought to have been embarrassed at such an encounter with honourable and decent people in such an unfortunate position. We ourselves were, however, anxious and tense with the responsibility of the situation. We knew that it was in all our interests that these men should simply go away, and now that they seemed prepared to do so we thought it impossibly good luck. They stood silently in the shade of the wall and trees. They each wore a multi-coloured Kashmiri scarf wound as a turban round their heads, all had beards, some black, many orange-red with henna dye, some few were white and wispy. They were mostly tall, for Omanis tend to height. Their eyes looked down and they scarcely spoke.

Shaikh Sultan passed the word to them that they were to lay their arms down in the sand. Nothing happened. He spoke again and one of his men ran up the line. It was a very tense moment, and the atmosphere was brittle. For a tribesman to give up his arms was akin to giving up his life, and only in hopeless circumstances, when leadership is absent, will they do this. As the word passed a second time, the first man stepped a pace forward and put his Lee Enfield on the sand in front of us. Shaikh Sultan bin Saif, bright and alert as ever, turned to me and said, 'Do not worry, my friend, all will be well.' He looked as if a great weight of responsibility had fallen from his shoulders, he smiled and the little creases at the corners of his temples tightened. He was happy, and I knew that for the moment, at least, we had gained our immediate objective.

Soon all the rifles were laid out in front of us, roughly in a line. Some were British Lee Enfield of various vintages, some were Mauser, and one of these pieces, a remarkable one, was a muzzle loader of enormous length with a smooth bore. This would have done us no harm, but the others were serious weapons to be reckoned with.

I called to our drivers and asked them to load these weapons into one of our lorries. This they did. Shaikh Sultan then spoke to our most experienced driver, an Omani who knew the camel-caravan route to Nizwa, and arranged with him that the arms would be unloaded by a certain tree about five miles away on the camel track. Then he asked Saifyan and one of his men to get into the truck and ride as far as the tree, then they were to get down and stay with the weapons to act as guards for them. They climbed into the truck and went off, and as soon as it had disappeared, Shaikh Sultan told the garrison to walk on after them. After a few words the unhappy group walked off up the *wadi* in the wake of the vehicle and their arms.

Looking back it is easier to assess the historical significance of such moments, but even at that time we were conscious that we had reached a turning point in the history of Oman. The Sultan of Muscat and Oman at that moment had become the direct Ruler of much of the interior, and certainly its deserts. Whether oil flowed or not, a political advance of importance had been made; and if oil were found, it would be as a result of that day's work. I could see no prospect of obtaining the necessary conditions for search and production of oil if Oman were allowed to break up into separate parts, as it had seemed to be on the point of doing. With the knowledge of what has happened since, I think that there can be little doubt that if Talib had continued his attempt at a separatist movement and dragged the Duru with him, against their will, the modern development of the whole state of Oman which the oil revenue now makes possible, would have been delayed for very many years.

What was uppermost in my mind at that time was the terrible position of the inhabitants of this remote area. The bedouin really lived at below subsistence level, infant mortality was very high, young men and women aged quickly and were senile in what we call middle age. They had virtually no property and for food relied almost entirely on dates. Rice and meat were a great rarity, a little fruit was available in the markets in early summer, and some vegetables in the villages; but in the desert they lived almost entirely on dates and camels' milk. Once the shaikhs had explained the reasons for our coming, the bedouin had become extraordinarily friendly; and we found them amusing and pleasant company. Of course they saw me as a source of money, and who can blame them for making the most of an opportunity; but when the immediate crisis passed off and we had no need of an irregular force, their importunities slackened. The people of Ibri itself were slightly better off than the desert folk, and after the fort had been surrendered they showered embarrassing hospitality upon us; for these people who have so little are generous with what they do have.

After the truck had driven away with the arms, and the garrison had walked off up the *wadi* bed and disappeared, Percy Coriat had them discreetly followed and observed until after they had picked up their arms and continued some miles on their way towards Nizwa. Shaikh Sultan called me and we went into one of the neighbouring date groves and we sat down on a tree trunk to talk it over. 'Oh my friend,' he said, 'God had willed that a good thing should happen here.' But, he added with a smile, 'He would wish us to make certain of it and, God willing, we can do what is needed. Those people of Talib's have now gone from here, but we must be sure that all the towns and villages of this region will reject the Imam if he tries to return; and above all we must make sure of Dariz and the valley leading from there to the Wadi Hawasini where my people are. Then we will have consolidated this area. You must at once persuade the Colonel to do what is necessary to bring this about. Patrols to the villages are essential. Will you do this?'

I did not explain that the Company headquarters, situated in the mezzanine and other higher floors of Peter Robinson's in Oxford Street, would have had a fit at such a proposal, and would fire me at once; but I said that of course I agreed, it was just what I was thinking myself. We then discussed the problem in more detail. The fort of Ainain, the large village of Dariz, the twin villages al-Araqi, the fort and village of Silaif, and the village of Bat, all these must declare against Talib and for the Sultan if any stability were to be gained; and we in Ibri must be ready to withstand if need be a counter-attack from hundreds of irregular tribesmen within perhaps two weeks. If we could cover all these points the immediate future was reasonably secure. If not we would be in trouble and could as easily lose all that we had gained.

I readily agreed with Shaikh Sultan's appreciation; and with his help I put on paper an assessment of the local tribal position as he then saw it. I had come armed with all the information which I could obtain from existing written records and I had in addition been interrogating any bedouin I met over a period of some months, but Shaikh Sultan bin Saif's balanced appreciation of the current political position among the tribes and his assessment of the strength and reliability of the shaikhs was essential as a basis for future planning.

After the garrison had left we sat talking in the shade of the trees, and one of his followers would now and then bring us bedouin coffee or sweet tea to refresh us. I said that patrols laid on systematically under his direction were the obvious solution, but I doubted if we could do it so simply. Let him arrange to visit all the leading shaikhs in each village, I would go with him and we would ask the MFF for protection. Shaikh Sultan smiled at this suggestion, but readily agreed. The afternoon of 27 October was a happy one in the history of Ibri. At about five o'clock Shaikh Sultan and I broke off our talk and we met Muhammed bin Abdullah by the edge of the town near where the garrison had surrendered, and with the shaikhs and many of the Duru followers made our way to the fort. Our companions and the townspeople were all excited, and as we approached the fort loosed off their rifles in all directions.

The joyous way in which we all entered the fort to a fusillage of small arms was much the most dangerous part of the day's proceedings. The fort is large and rambling with very thick walls, and although its courtyards could be dominated by troops on the surrounding height, its

towers have thick walls and narrow slit windows; it was quite obvious
that the garrison could easily have kept our small force out of the fort as
long as their food and water lasted. But stocks of both we found were very
low. It must have been partly this and partly the low morale which
induced the surrender.

In the courtyard we were shown the gun, a big muzzle loader with a
bore of some three or four inches, which stood ready loaded pointing
roughly to the main MFF position. From the way it was sited I doubted
if the large ball would have cleared the wall of the fort. The ball was then
removed and the barrel packed with rubbish and the gun fired in
celebration. It made a rather feeble boom, but with a great deal of smoke
and flame. This was accompanied by cheers and many more shots from
our Duru irregulars.

The MFF took up position on the heights and built rough defensive
positions, *sangars*, there. We did not expect any immediate counter-
attack from Talib since he had no motor transport at all, and his main
force was reported to be in Rustaq, but after a week or so we thought it
likely that he would make some move against us. Percy Coriat made a
strong point with slit-trenches by the *wadi* just north of the gap in the
hills through which the *wadi* runs. After two nights spent in the date
grove he said he could not guarantee our safety unless we moved into the
strong-point area. He was right to move us, although I could not see that
he was in a position to guarantee our safety wherever we were. However,
we complied and a very uncomfortable time we had, since we still had no
tents, but some camp beds had now been sent up. Angus had gone back
to Duqm and among other things organized traffic along our now very
lengthy supply route. Our water supply was perfectly satisfactory for as
long as we stayed in Ibri where there was plenty, but all petrol and food
had to come from Duqm; and the convoys took two or even three days, as
many of the vehicles were by now giving trouble after the bashing the
desert tracks had given them (and us!)

I suffered an attack of malaria accompanied by dysentery, and being
confined during day-time to a camp bed under the narrow shade of a
palm tree, with the air temperature in the shade around 100°F, was far
from amusing, and to keep in the shade meant moving my bed every half
an hour or so. Moreover the bedouin kept visiting me, and although I
had paid off the private army of the Duru, bedouin came flocking in
looking for 'help'. Our strong-point camp was very congested and I

longed for the peace afforded by desert camp life, and its comparative privacy. These were trying days.

Shaikh Sultan bin Saif was now more worried than ever that so many surrounding villages had not yet declared their allegiance to the Sultan of Muscat. They needed a little more encouragement, and if we dared not visit them they would assume we were afraid of Talib; this would prevent them showing their hand in favour of the Sultan. Shaikh Sultan thought he should call on them, but, as I had feared, we were told that the MFF would not be allowed to go with him; if I were to go, according to the curious rules of the game which we were playing, they would have to come. Percy had confirmed this rather reluctantly; but he was firm that he should not on his own initiative send out patrols. 'After all I should not be here at all, and when the Sultan hears, I shall get the most fearful rocket, old boy!'

Accordingly on 31 October Shaikh Sultan bin Saif and I set off in my Land Rover followed by the MFF platoon in trucks which was under the command of Major Mike O'Kelly. I had heard so much of these places near Ibri that I was now excited to see them. When you have talked and talked about places, discussed the personalities and allegiance of their shaikhs, and discussed the relative strength and importance of their forts, one has a picture of them and it is fascinating to see the reality. Our first objective was the Arab part of al-Araqi village, a group of habitations that was half-Baluch, half-Arab. We had some reason to believe the Arab shaikh had now declared his loyalty to the Sultan; but when we approached we saw no reassuring red flag flying on the north-eastern quarter.

At the end of the village we stopped our vehicles and Shaikh Sultan, myself and a few of his followers went forward on foot. As we came round the corner of the first house we could see, by the entrance to the fort, and in its courtyard, a group of armed men. Shaikh Sultan said, 'Watch out, these are the Imam's people.' He bravely held his ground while I went back to shout to Mike O'Kelly to ask him to come to our aid. This Mike very quickly did, and at once came up to the fort at the head of two sections carrying Brens and rifles. The appearance of the troops enabled Sultan to persuade the 'enemy' to withdraw. He at once called the shaikh of the village and asked him to find some friendly armed men to man the fort. He soon collected ten villagers whose loyalty he trusted and we saw them go into the fort.

The waiting period while the 'enemy' were removed and friends put in their place was filled as usual with the drinking of coffee and tea. Rugs were spread for us in the courtyard of the main fort and we were able to watch the unusual scene in comfort. It was not unlike a Shakespearean play in which the enemy are on one side of the stage, and the supposedly 'good' people of the play on the other, at one and the same time, seemingly unaware of each other's presence. But this was reality not a scene on a stage. The atmosphere in the fort was extremely tense, and there was little conversation, but both Mike O'Kelly and Shaikh Sultan bin Saif managed to look very relaxed. I suppose the little drama took no more than fifteen minutes.

I was extremely relieved when Shaikh Sultan declared that we could now safely move on, as the well-disposed people were firmly established, their shaikh professing utmost loyalty to the Sultan, and the 'enemy' had just departed (having had coffee of course). Our next objective was the great fort of Ainain, which, as its name indicates, sits astride the line of two water channels. Its domination of the water channels, which are the sources of water for Ibri and al-Araqi, gives it importance and this and its size ensures for it a special significance in terms of old fashioned tribal fighting. It would, of course, be hopelessly vulnerable to modern artillery or rocket attack but to such weapons as were available at that time to the Omanis, it was virtually impregnable.

The fortress lies near al-Araqi in the middle of the small plain at either end of which are Ibri and Dariz. Making a circuit of the gardens of al-Araqi we took a winding path to it among the stunted trees and bushes that are typical of the area of the foothills. The plain was still and silent, and the morning air rather oppressive. Mike O'Kelly now decided to keep right up with us in case, despite Shaikh Sultan's assurances, there were some of the enemy in Ainain as well, and we advanced roughly in line abreast. As we drew close to the fort we could see His Highness the Sultan's red flag flying from the upper turret. We were, however, met by a fusillade of shots, and Mike and I both stopped our vehicles. 'Go on, go on,' said Shaikh Sultan in genuine surprise and concern, 'this is their way of welcoming us.' We should have known better I suppose, but it does take some getting used to.

Welcome indeed it was. Several men came running out of the main door with shouts and broad smiles to greet us. Their leader was the son of the Shaikh of Dariz. The shaikh had been forced to acknowledge Ghalib when the Imam's army came through, and had had to quarter some of them in his village. But he had considered himself powerless to resist. He was, therefore, forced to raise the Imam's white flag on Ainain fort, and instructed his son, who usually held that place on his father's behalf, to recognize the Imam and his brother when they came here. This he had naturally been obliged to do.

When the Shaikh of Dariz heard that Ibri had fallen and heard the news of the departure on foot of the garrison, he decided that he could safely show his allegiance to His Highness the Sultan, and sent messengers to Shaikh Sultan bin Saif to this effect. The flag on Ainain had then been changed again, and his son was ordered to welcome us and accompany us to Dariz whenever we should appear. From Ainain's ramparts we could see Dariz clearly across the plain a few miles away and we looked eagerly at its fort to see what kind of flag was flying. Through Mike's binoculars it looked much nearer to white than red, but we could not be sure. The Shaikh's son laughed when questioned on this all-important point, and said, 'Yes, father's flags have all faded and he gave me the reddest one as this fort would be the first you would reach.'

He then assured us he would go with us to see his father. I was relieved at this since despite Shaikh Sultan bin Saif's assurances and apparent readiness to take risks, I was beginning to feel less than keen to accompany him to each new place, unless we had with us some of the people of the shaikh concerned.

After coffee we set off with the young shaikh sitting in the Land Rover between Shaikh Sultan bin Saif and myself. This time we all drove straight up to the fort in a close group. There was no firing and no excitement; very few people were about in the narrow streets between the square mud houses. The young shaikh ran in to get his father and we waited outside. The old man came out almost at once, a dignified figure with a white beard and wrinkled smiling face, and greeted Sultan Saif warmly with the bedouin embrace and touching of noses; then he asked us all in to his *majlis*. Mike first posted his soldiers and then joined us.

We were entertained with coffee, tea and hot milk with cinnamon. The room was quite a large one, furnished as is so usual in that area, with Persian and Baluchi carpets. As we sat talking, more and more of the villagers came in and we stood to shake hands with each group. The shaikh then invited us to lunch. As it was only eleven in the morning, and Sultan Saif said lunch could not be prepared in less than two or three hours, as the sheep would not have been killed yet, I suggested that we should visit the Baluchi quarter at al-Araqi first and then return. This was agreed.

Shaikh Sultan bin Saif's tactics with regard to the Baluch were as follows. He doubted whether they would readily accept the allegiance of the Sultan of Muscat. This particular section of the Baluch have been in the area many years. Although their ancestors originated in Baluchistan those in the interior of Oman speak Arabic and dress and live as Arabs. The village had rather a reputation for opposition to the Muscat government. Over the last thirty years, this had meant little, and there had been no actual fighting between the Baluch and other Omanis but Shaikh Sultan bin Saif thought that the arrival of uniformed soldiers from Muscat, for the first time in history, might cause trouble. I had no reason to disagree with this assessment; and as with all our dealings with tribes, relied on his judgement. Shaikh Sultan thought that now that Ibri, Ainain, Dariz and the Arab quarter of al-Araqi were flying the Sultan's governmental flag, the Baluch, who were small in numbers, would have no option but to follow suit. This seemed a logical argument, and it had been for this reason that he had by-passed this village and left it to the last of this group.

We advanced in our trucks to within two hundred yards of the Baluchi village. All was quiet, no flag was flying and no people were in sight. The son of the Shaikh of Dariz had come with us, and Shaikh Sultan also had several men from Ibri with him. He calculated that the presence of the shaikh's son would prevent any trouble, since if the Baluch fired on any party of which this man was a member, they would at once be at feud with the people of Dariz. Ainain fort was astride the main part of the village water supply and the position of the inhabitants of al-Araqi would be impossible if they were at war with whoever held Ainain. This sounded all very reasonable, but I said I did not feel like driving straight into al-Araqi without Mike and the MFF, nor did I even much like the obvious alternative of going in with the troops since this would almost certainly prove to be provocative. So we discussed what we should do.

Shaikh Sultan bin Saif was the most accommodating of men. He may have thought me a little unhelpful not to drive in with him, but he agreed at once that it was unsafe for any of us to go in; and even added, perhaps as a sop to our conscience, that the presence of Europeans at the first instance might produce the wrong effect. The Baluch might feel entitled to fire at foreigners, whoever was with them, and they were likely to resent uniforms even more.

Shaikh Sultan bin Saif said, 'I will go in with my party on foot. If I do not come out within ten minutes you are free to take what action you like, but I am sure it will be all right.' The patrol had drawn up some two hundred yards from the houses. Shaikh Sultan bin Saif gathered his men and set off on foot into the village. They disappeared round the corner of a house and then there was silence. Mike deployed his men, and we sat and waited. Although Sultan Saif had seemed so confident I was worried about him, and I wondered how on earth we could rescue him if he met resistance since we had a force of merely twenty-five men and two Bren guns. We waited a full ten minutes with no sounds except the common noises of an Omani village, the ever-present squeak of a well pulley, the cries of poultry and the periodic noise of water swishing into the water channel from the leather bucket that is pulled by the ox. Then round the corner of the house came one of Shaikh Sultan bin Saif's men. He ran over to us and said in some excitement that Shaikh Sultan had been well received and he was trying to persuade the shaikh, Rashid bin Said of the Baluch, to come out to meet us. But he did not want us to go into the village.

We all felt better after hearing this news, but we were kept waiting another half-hour before we saw the squat figure of Shaikh Sultan bin Saif coming out from among the houses accompanied by the white-bearded Shaikh Rashid of the Baluch and several followers from each side. The shaikhs came very slowly towards us. I thought that our soldiers in what was their inevitably offensive looking positions behind Brens and rifles had something less than a friendly air. Perhaps this was what was upsetting the shaikh. When he finally came up to us the old shaikh looked far from pleased. We shook hands. He said very simply, with or without irony I shall never know, 'I acknowledge my loyalty to His Highness the Sultan as ever before.' Not much more was said, the shaikh took his leave and walked back to the village. Mike ordered his troops into the trucks and we drove back to Dariz. No flag, however, flew over the Baluch quarter of al-Araqi; 'Perhaps he hasn't got one' said Sultan Saif with a smile.

At Dariz we found the whole village in a festive mood. We were immediately invited into the main *majlis* of the fort where the shaikh greeted us warmly. We all sat down and had coffee amidst a buzz of friendly conversation. We described our visit to al-Araqi and the shaikh laughed hugely when we told him how glum Shaikh Rashid had been. Sultan Saif warned me that lunch was still not ready and recommended a walk round the village to look at the farms. This was agreed and we were made very welcome and given coffee and tea and yet more hot camel's milk and cinnamon by several villagers in their houses. Then we were summoned back to the fort where a large meal was spread out on rugs and sheets in the open under the trees.

I was placed between Shaikh Sultan bin Saif and the old Shaikh of Dariz. We talked of tribal matters, and, knowing that his tribe, originally Bani Ghafir, was commonly known as the Miyayaha, I said in all innocence, '*Inta Miyahi*,' meaning, 'You are a Miyahi' (or a tribesman from the Miyayaha). This produced guffaws of laughter, but the shaikh looked very embarrassed, and I changed the subject. Sultan Saif afterwards explained to me that the word Miyayaha (adjective Miyahi) means changing of sides and was used as a name for this section of the Bani Ghafir because it changed its faction. Thus to say what I said really meant, 'You are a changer of sides.' As he had changed the colour of his flag only that day, this was felt to be much too apt, and accounted for the way in which his followers had dissolved in laughter. Sultan Saif had guessed that I had not meant it that way, and that I did not understand the meaning of the name, but doubtless the others thought I had done it on purpose; and if ever afterwards I wanted to make Sultan Saif laugh I had only to remind him of this gaffe of mine. We returned to Ibri well satisfied with a good day's work.

My opinion of Shaikh Sultan bin Saif's judgement and ability had already been high, and now it was looking as if he were nearly infallible on tribal affairs. I also thought he had shown great courage in going into al-Araqi on his own. We were still worried about Silaif. Our information was that the fort was unoccupied, and the villagers loyal to the Sultan. It was said that some six people had been killed in the original attack on Silaif, and although it did not look likely that there would be another attack on the place immediately, it did seem only prudent to make sure of it, as later the Imam might try to seize it as a prelude to an attack on Ibri. This seemed to be a standard practice for anyone wishing to take Ibri, and it would prove very embarrassing to us if he did this again.

Percy Coriat did not altogether agree on its military importance, but I pointed out that, in these tribal affairs, it is only what seems to be of importance to the tribes that matters, never mind orthodox military principles. They usually run their tribal affairs by accepted rules, rather like a game of chess, and casualties are kept to a minimum if the rules are observed. If a large force presents itself before a village, the village usually surrenders, since it can do so without loss of face. This is really the secret of such skirmishing. If certain forts are captured the allegiance of a whole region can be changed. It is, however, vital to capture all the right forts. Therefore, we should anticipate Talib's moves and make moves to counter them; and when he heard of the action we had taken it would, I hoped, discourage him altogether from attacking in this area. If we left key forts empty it would be an open invitation. This was the very mistake Talib had made and which enabled us to come in.

However, Percy was quite right in refusing to put any of his own men into Silaif. It is a good military principle to keep a small force concentrated, and he still had only one hundred and twenty-six men up with him in the Ibri area. I tried to persuade Shaikh Sultan bin Saif to collect loyal irregulars to garrison Silaif. Shaikh Sultan had no authority from his master to do anything, except to assist the Company; he still had no government money, but I could lend him cash, hoping we would be repaid by the Muscat government later. He was, therefore, in a delicate position, not knowing for certain the wishes of the Sultan of Muscat five hundred miles away, but guessing disapproval of such tactics. Yet he agreed at length to my proposal.

The following day, again with Mike O'Kelly and a platoon, we went to Silaif. The villagers streamed out to greet us and assured us that the fort was without a garrison. The door of the fort was in fact wide open and there was no one in it. Silaif fort is in a commanding position some four miles south-east of Ibri on the same ridge that skirts the north of the latter town. The fort is built at another break in the ridge similar to the gorge at Ibri. It is partly built on a low cliff and with curtain walls which straggle up the hill and reminded me of those at Antioch, but on a much smaller scale. Our ten men, whom we had taken up for the purpose, could not hope to hold it against a force of any size, but they might prevent a small force from getting into it, and this was all Shaikh Sultan could manage for a time. Percy Coriat promised to send patrols to it periodically in order to encourage its defenders.

The valley system of which Ibri and Dariz form the centre, had now become a bloc in which all the people with the exception of those in a village called Bat, had acknowledged the Sultan. Shaikh Rashid of the Baluch controlled all the other Baluch villages to the west. We counted on Ainain fort and its commanding position over the water channels to keep him in line. Bat village was at a point which commanded an important valley on one of the routes to the east and, to complete the job of assuring allegiance of the shaikhs of the key places, it was essential to visit this village and persuade its shaikh to show his hand.

On 3 November Shaikh Sultan bin Saif, Mike O'Kelly and I went to Bat with this aim, accompanied by a patrol of MFF. Shaikh Sultan wanted all of us to stay outside the village to begin with as the situation might become delicate, he thought; therefore, we halted on a prominent little hill near the village and sent in on foot an emissary to explain our presence and our aims.

He returned some time later with a village notable called Salim who was under instructions from the elderly, indeed senile, village shaikh, to discuss the question of allegiance with Shaikh Sultan, and go with us to Ibri for the purpose. They seemed prepared to accept His Highness the Sultan as their Ruler, but he wished for an adequate force to overawe the village in order to make his submission appear not too readily given. As they correctly considered they were unable to defend themselves from the Imam's army, they had ample justification for seeking an insurance policy to protect themselves from Talib's wrath, had they deserted him too willingly.

In the event, by delaying a day, they lost their chance of appearing to submit to a sizeable force. The patrol that went with us on 3 November had consisted of some twenty men. By the time we got back to Ibri we discovered that Percy Coriat had received fresh orders by radio from Salalah reiterating that he was to send no patrols at all. I explained to him how serious it would be politically if Bat did not acknowledge the Sultan and at least by implication disavow the Imam; but the best I could get from him was the promise of an escort of two soldiers for myself and Shaikh Sultan bin Saif, if we were unwise enough to visit Bat again contrary to his advice. Percy now had his radio working, connecting him with Duqm and thus in turn Salalah, and he could get in touch with the Sultan again; but the Sultan, who had disapproved very strongly of our entry into Ibri, could not be persuaded by radio messages that the policy we were following was not only right but was proving a great success. Direct contact with his master now tied Percy's hands completely.

The interdiction on patrolling not only put an end to moves designed to secure the extension of the Sultanate's direct authority in the whole Ibri area, but it also brought to an end a plan we had formulated for obtaining the allegiance of the shaikhs of Dhank, a place some forty miles to the north. We had already been in touch with some of the leaders from Dhank who had come into Ibri. Dhank is an important communications centre, only a little less significant politically than Ibri itself; and it was a pity we could not do anything there. As it turned out its shaikhs did not formally acknowledge the direct rule of the Sultan for a further year.

Salim turned out to be an extremely reasonable and intelligent man; sent by his shaikh with instructions to negotiate for a larger force than the twenty which had first come to the village on 3 November, he in the end found himself being talked into accepting a ridiculous 'force' of only two soldiers. At first he would of course have none of it, but the irony of the situation must have so fascinated him, he started to laugh and then decided to agree. 'But,' he said, 'it must be first thing tomorrow, since I shall have to convince my shaikh that I was given no alternative. If I were to tell him this in advance, he would start to argue and then we should never get anywhere; and what is more, we shall have to enter Bat together.' Shaikh Sultan and I discussed the wisdom of this after Salim had agreed to our proposal. Shaikh Sultan thought it would be all right. I reluctantly agreed. 'Moreover,' said Shaikh Sultan, 'if it works it could prove a great gain, as it will show that in fact no pressure is needed to induce admission of allegiance to the Sultan.' This was an important point, but was the risk worth taking? By strong contrast, when they had earlier submitted to Ghalib and Talib, the Imam had with him a force reputed to be of four hundred men, that mystic figure.

We parted for the night chuckling at the ironical turns which this little affair seemed to be taking and, having arranged for our 'escort' to parade at sunrise, we went to sleep on it.

We set out the following morning in three vehicles (one would have carried us all, but three looked so much better) and we reached the neighbourhood of Bat still in the cool of the morning. On this occasion, as we had previously agreed, we all drove in together. From the very first, as soon as we reached the houses, we were welcomed with the greatest possible warmth and friendliness. The old shaikh, too decrepit to walk, could barely stand to greet us; but he received us in front of his unpretentious mud-brick house, surrounded by all the men of the village.

We were invited to lunch, but excused ourselves and instead were entertained with tea, coffee, fruit and cheese, dishes on as lavish a scale as the place could provide; and it was after mid-day before we could get away. Salim seemed to have great influence over the shaikh and his elders, and his first words had been sufficient to persuade them to accept the *fait accompli* with as brave a face as possible, despite the disadvantage that this proclaimed to the country at large, and the Imam in particular, how genuine was their loyalty to the Sultan.

Salim came back with us to Ibri to stay another night as the guest of Shaikh Mohammad of the Yaaqib, who arranged a celebration dinner for us all that evening. Shaikh Sultan bin Saif and I felt rather pleased with ourselves, and we all had a good time that evening with considerable laughter and fun, and perhaps too much mutual congratulation. These days of patrols up the valley were interspersed with much feasting in Ibri. The villagers vied with one another to have Shaikh Sultan to meals in their houses. We continued to live in the palm-grove to the north of the town, but at meal times, when I was not out on patrol, we would find ourselves in one or other of the houses. As the weather was still hot, meals would usually be spread out under an awning in the courtyard. We would sit on rugs, with cushions between each guest and his neighbour. Twenty or thirty, sometimes many more, would sit round each meal, which invariably consisted of mounds of beautifully cooked rice surmounted by whole sheep or goats. Little dishes of cheese, tomatoes and fruit would be round the main dish.

I now saw two further desirable purely political aims. The first was to go through to the Wadi Hawasini where, naturally, all the tribesmen owed direct loyalty to Shaikh Sultan bin Saif, their paramount, and therefore to the Sultan of Muscat himself; this would join up a good slice of the country and above all give direct access through the mountain chain to the sea from the potential oilfield area. It would get round the difficulty that Talib could probably control all the outer mountain passes between the likely oil area and the sea. The second was to make sure of Dhank in order to give the Sultan complete and direct control again of the whole of the area of the Dhahirah plain up to Buraimi.

These were obvious things to do. However, the new orders received by Coriat made any further move by us impossible. I therefore arranged, through the Company, that Shaikh Sultan bin Saif would fly to Dhufar in order to explain to His Highness the Sultan in person how things had gone with us and explain what he, Shaikh Sultan bin Saif, thought needed to be done now. I hoped that this visit would persuade the Sultan to delegate authority properly to the shaikh and appoint him his official representative for this operation at least. Shaikh Sultan bin Saif thought it better if I did not go with him. I think he was right.

Nick Fallan had meanwhile chosen an airstrip near Ibri to the east, and measured it; and I, rather light-heartedly, at his suggestion marked it out by the simple expedient of towing the trunk of a palm tree behind a Land Rover along each of its sides. The tree made a clear yellow cut in the grey gravel surface, and showed from the air as a yellow line. I believe our strip is still in use as the airfield. We were, therefore, able to ask the Company for an aeroplane, and in due course, a Dove came. I took the opportunity of its arrival to give Shaikh Sultan bin Saif, Shaikh Muhammad bin Abdullah and some of the Duru shaikhs a ride in it, and persuaded the very co-operative pilot, on the excuse that our guests wished to see their own villages, to give them a tour round a very much larger area than the one which had given allegiance to the Sultan. Shaikh Sultan bin Saif then quite unknown to me arranged for it to be put about as local gossip that our innocent little ten-seater De Havilland Dove was both a bomber and a fighter of great power and speed.

At a luncheon party given afterwards by the Shaikh of Ibri, in honour of his colleagues and our pilot, one of the elderly bedouin shaikhs who had been for a ride in the Dove said, 'I want a machine like that for myself.' It took quite a bit of questioning to discover that he was not referring to the aircraft at all, but to the Land Rover which had taken him to it. It transpired that he thought the aircraft rather ordinary, since he had already seen them flying overhead; and he also thought aircraft would be too complicated; whereas the motor vehicles, which were really new to him, he thought more wonderful, and more suitable. Like some of the others, his first ride in a car took place on the same day as his first ride in the air.

Regretfully we began to unravel the arrangements we had made in regard to Dhank, while awaiting news of Shaikh Sultan bin Saif's important trip to Salalah. Meanwhile Shaikh Zayed, who had been hunting in the Wadi al-Amairi, visited us and his arrival was the occasion for great rejoicing and much feasting, for he was very popular and the biggest personality throughout the Dhahirah.

Although Shaikh Zayed had no responsibility himself at all in the Ibri area, the Sultan had welcomed his co-operation in the Dhahirah, and I thought that his appearance now would have a stabilizing effect. This proved to be the case. Shaikh Zayed always showed an interest in the welfare of his neighbours in Oman. Provided the Company was doing its best to find oil in Abu Dhabi (and it was doing so) he was anxious to see it working also in neighbouring Oman. It was a great pleasure to see Shaikh Zayed and his brother Shaikh Hizza in Ibri, and all the town rejoiced. Lunch and dinner were occasions for entertaining them for three days, and they in return entertained at their desert camp just outside the town.

There was one particular party given by the townsmen, in which the warmth and friendliness of our hosts were as great as usual, but in which I had a curious experience. Our hosts had over-extended themselves in the interests of hospitality, a worthy motive. They offered us a camel, sheep and chickens all cooked with rice, served at about 10 a.m. in the open; just before the feast a wind came up which served both to cool the meal and to spread over it a layer of fine sand. As we squatted round it, my neighbour advised me to dig deep into the pile with my right hand, sound advice, since only thus could rice be found that was still warm and free of sand. I was getting on well, but in the process came upon the fingers of the man opposite who was doing the same. It was a little unnerving to find something moving amidst the rice.

These meals were fine ones, when there was no dust blowing, the meat and rice being beautifully cooked. Hosts and guests were able to enjoy themselves, and after a cup of coffee the party would split up into groups. It was an easy and pleasant form of entertainment for the guests; but it must call for very hard work from the hosts, and for the tribesmen and shaikhs it meant a great expenditure. The cordiality of these meetings underlines the notion that to break bread or partake of salt is a very real expression of friendship and a ritual to celebrate the forgetting of any differences. These desert scenes were part of an age-old tradition.

Shaikh Sultan bin Saif, and a little later Percy Coriat, made their visits to Dhufar and saw His Highness the Sultan who, when he had heard the full story, reluctantly, and with bad grace, accepted what had happened so far. Although he said he disagreed with our methods he never attempted to explain how he thought we could have done otherwise if we had hoped to achieve our objectives. But he maintained his veto on any further adventures.

The consequences of the re-occupation of Ibri by the Omani central government were far-reaching. The Company drilled at Fahud, but not quite in the right place. IPC then relinquished the concession which was taken up by Shell, Total and the Gulbenkian Foundation, constituting a new company called Petroleum Development Oman (PDO). This new company drilled a little further up the Fahud anticlinal structure and found oil in commercial quantities. Meanwhile the Sultan had established his government in Nizwa over all Oman only to lose control temporarily of a part of the interior with the revolt by Talib and Ghalib in 1957. However, he regained his position with the aid of a small body of British, mainly SAS, in 1958. Oil was first exported by PDO in 1963. In 1970 Saiyyid Qaboos deposed his father and immediately set about the task of reform and master-minded development in Oman at great speed with the remarkable results one can see today. But this great sucess could never have happened had Ibri not been occupied by our little expedition in October 1954, as Talib and Ghalib would have increased their power and the whole state of Oman would have been dismembered within months. Our expedition, therefore, had the happiest results and events unfolded in the way that the Sultan and the directors of the IPC had envisaged in the planning stage. The Sultan himself, however, in the autumn of 1954 had come near to frustrating all our efforts with his letter to me prohibiting our entry into the area where the oil was later found. Only two of the more adventurous shareholders who formed PDO succeeded in winning the prize they had worked so hard for. But that was to look forward six years.

Meanwhile I remained in Ibri for several more days, unable to get about much because of fresh attacks of malaria and dysentery. At the same time the geologists established a camp near Fahud. I was helped over this period by Stewart Watt, a delightful and very able colleague from the Company, who joined us, and when I finally left in late 1954 on the orders of the Company doctor, he took over responsibility for the political side from me.

12

Excitement in Buraimi

The winter 1954-5 was something of a break in my way of life. When my health had improved I was suddenly moved by the Company to Bahrain, then to Qatar, and then on to Kirkuk in northern Iraq. This move to Kirkuk was explained to me by the personnel people of the Company, as designed to turn me into a respectable oil man. The IPC (Iraq Petroleum Company) was Kirkuk, and Kirkuk was the IPC; anyone who had not served for many years in Iraq or possibly in Syria, where the pipe-line terminated, was not a proper Company man, and I had to learn about oil. I thought that I was already learning a great deal about the exploration side as I used often to travel with the geologists, writing their notes for them, as they clambered on the rocks, or listening to their discussions back at our camp. I had also learned something about seismic work and drilling. This was not considered anything and I was to go to Kirkuk as a new boy. New boys in the Company usually came to Iraq straight from the UK as beginners, but I had already behind me a dozen years of experience in the Middle East and several years in the Company of much harder living and more varied Company work than many of the men in Kirkuk would have experienced. To be treated in this way, my friends in the Company warned me before I left, would not be much fun. It was not.

After three weeks I found the job so trivial and boring and myself so unwanted that I was just settling down to write a letter of resignation when a message came from the personnel office that they wanted to see me. I was told by a very nice, but clearly astonished, head of personnel, that he had just received a telegram from London posting me back to Bahrain, and I was to go there at once with all my goods and chattels.

During the next few months which I spent partly in the oil camp in Qatar and partly in Bahrain and the Trucial Coast, I was directly responsible to Heseldin. I found this a great deal easier than when I had been working through others at a distance, and by this time it was apparent that he took what I said about the political position without question. The change was extraordinary. I had a great deal of travelling to do round the lower Gulf and I was, by now, fit. So I found myself once again, among other things, studying the familiar old problem of the Saudi claim to Abu Dhabi and Omani territory; the 'Buraimi' problem, as it was always called by the British and the Americans. I could see this as a struggle in the first place between oil companies, with governments becoming more and more involved.

The history of Buraimi, the oasis and its problem are important. As far as records go back the oasis was a border one between Oman and the Northern Shaikhdoms. In the nineteenth century the Abu Dhabi shaikhs consolidated their position in the six villages on the al-Ain side of the oasis, while the Omanis (the Naim and Al Bu Shams tribes) occupied the three villages centred on Buraimi itself, the other two being Saarah and Hamasah. The Saudis had occupied some of the villages on the Omani side for thirteen short periods, from 1800 until 1869, when the then Imam of Muscat, Azzan bin Qais, drove them out. They never occupied them again. The British Government in India had strong treaty relations with the Trucial Shaikhdoms from 1820, and there were very friendly ties with Muscat and Oman dating back to 1798, although in this case defence was not specifically mentioned. The British did not interfere with the various Saudi occupations of the Omani villages in the nineteenth century but on several occasions they warned the Saudi Emir of their special relationship with the Trucial shaikhs, and in response the latter promised to respect the position of those shaikhs who had this treaty relationship with Britain and they did respect it. There is no record of their occupying the villages on the Abu Dhabi side. When they finally left in 1869, control of the Buraimi side of the oasis reverted once more to Oman.

In the twenties and thirties Saudi itinerant tax collectors on camels occasionally trespassed into parts of the Abu Dhabi desert, collecting the *Zakat*, or religious alms, but they did not do so in any settled place. As we may see from the habits of the bedouin, a tribesman intercepted by officials of the great King would feel he had to pay the religious tax – if he had any money – and in any case he would receive a present in cash from the tax collector, far greater than the sum he paid. Both the intimidation and the reward were more than enough to produce a modest payment by the bedouin and a thumbprint on any paper offered to him for signature. Thus the Saudis built up a record of tax collecting. The bedouin at that time knew about tribal areas (which often crossed international frontiers, e.g. the Ruwalla who move as a tribe annually between Syria, Jordan and Saudi Arabia), but such concepts as sovereignty, international frontiers, and nationality were unknown to them.

In August 1952 when, as I have mentioned, a small Saudi force entered Hamasah village at the invitation of its Shaikh Rashid bin Hamad of the Al Bu Shams, Shaikh Rashid's action was naturally named as high treason by the Sultan in Muscat. The paramount shaikh of the tribes centred on Buraimi, Saqr al-Naimi, held himself aloof, or tried to do so, but in the Sultan's eyes he was equally to blame. The Sultan and the Imam both raised large tribal forces and marched on Buraimi. They were stopped by the British Consul General who requested the Sultan in Suhar not to go any further. The Sultan reluctantly retired as did the Imam. The two forces were strong enough to have overwhelmed the Saudis who were few and not well armed. The Imam's army had reached Ibri and it alone could have decided the affair. This is the only case I know of, after the Sib Agreement of 1921, in which the Sultan and the Imam operated in concert militarily.

Then followed a Standstill Agreement in October 1952 and in 1954 an Abitration Agreement. By the latter the Saudis and the British Trucial Oman Levies, later to be called the Scouts, were each to maintain one officer and fifteen men in the oasis. The Saudis had the right to supply their small force by air, since no other means was practical. Each little force set up its camp near al-Ain; and the arbitration procedure, with judges chosen by each side to meet in Geneva, was set in motion. Her Majesty's Government, however, said that they had received clear proof of breaches of the agreement by the other party and two of the three judges had just resigned.

I was sitting at home in the Company house I was then using in Bahrain late one evening in October 1955 when the Political Resident Sir Bernard Burroughs asked to see me at the Residency. I drove over at once and Sir Bernard took me into his study to discuss a telegram he had just received. He stressed that what he had to say was secret. He said that HMG was about to abrogate the Buraimi Standstill Agreement uni-laterally because HMG claimed that the Saudis had breached it by their behaviour in regard to one of the judges. The Trucial Oman Levies were to go into the Buraimi zone on 25 October 1955. They would ask the Saudi contingent of fifteen police and the Saudi Emir to leave, and a plane would be there to take them away. They would be joined in the operation by the Omani army.

He asked me if I would be prepared to go into the Buraimi zone with the troops as his representative to persuade the inhabitants not to resist the entry either of the Trucial Levies or the Omani Army, and should they have done so before I could get there, to intervene and stop any fighting. The aim would be to persuade the shaikhs of Buraimi and Hamasah to go to Muscat and make their peace with the Sultan's government. The Sultan was still in Salalah. Sir Bernard said he would inform Colonel Johnson, Commander of the Levies, that I would be representing him and would be responsible for all political issues, thus in effect, for peace or war.

Sir Bernard kept emphasizing that HMG was most anxious to accomplish all this without any bloodshed, and two squadrons of Levies, about 220 men, were to go in by vehicle from Sharjah to do the operation. They planned to surround the Saudi contingent with an overwhelming force at first light, and then fly them out. This part of the operation would not present much difficulty it was thought. A contingent was also expected to come from the Omani Army, but it would not be there for the first few hours.

The real problem was that an unknown number of bedouin were in and around Hamasah. These were mainly Kaabis from Mahadah in the Sultanate (from just outside the Buraimi zone). They were all Sultanate subjects, but they supported Shaikh Rashid bin Hamad of Hamasah. It was feared that even after the Saudi contingent had left, these bedouin might remain in Hamasah and resist the entry of the Sultanate forces or, if they were involved, the Levies. Sir Bernard assured me that the Company in London had agreed to my being temporarily seconded for this operation.

I agreed to attempt this task, although I pointed out that I foresaw two difficulties. First, the force we could deploy did not look to me big enough to achieve our aim, but I was told no more troops were available. Second, I could not see the shaikhs, Saqr al-Naimi, Rashid bin Hamad, Obaid bin Juma and Mana bin Ali surrendering to the Sultan. Unless they were heavily outnumbered it looked as if they might fight. No sane person would willingly go to Muscat if that might mean Muscat gaol probably for life. Sir Bernard smiled, 'Do what you can,' he said. 'Those are the orders.'

We had no time to consider the finer points, since we had only forty-eight hours before the operation was to begin. My brief was to prevent bloodshed if I could and do my best to get the Sultanate shaikhs to surrender to the Sultan of Muscat. The following morning, 24 October 1955, I flew by RAF Dakota to Sharjah. After landing I went on to the station commander's office to finalize arrangements for the following morning. The Levies had already left in trucks for the so-called Buraimi zone and I was to join them by air on the 25th. Sabir had met me at the airstrip. It was not unusual for me to arrive by RAF since there were still few regular civilian flights and I sometimes came by RAF. I pretended to Sabir and to the staff at the Company house that I was on a normal visit on Company business, and as I had been making such visits so frequently there was nothing unusual about my appearance on this occasion.

Back at the Company house in Dubai I did some work and dined. That night to allay suspicion I ordered morning tea at 7 a.m. as usual, but by 4 a.m. I was driving the Company Humber over to Sharjah. The RAF promised to drive it back. I left a note in the Company office to tell the staff where I had gone. I was given an excellent breakfast at the airfield, cooked by the OC personally. On the strip was the solitary Dakota, and in the chill morning darkness I climbed aboard with a small suitcase. What I missed most was the presence of Shaikh Sultan bin Saif. Had he been with me I felt I should not have had much to worry about. I was the only passenger. We lumbered into the air and in just under an hour, as the sun was rising over the oasis, we came down towards the landing strip.

I was standing behind the Captain on the flight deck and we could see the airstrip marked with a line of oil drums, showing as a streak of light brown on the gravel plain. The radio operator tried to make contact with the Levies but could not do so. At the corner of Hamasah village there was a pall of white smoke and we could see a small group of vehicles by the palm trees of al-Jimi village. By the side of the airstrip stood a single Land Rover which I hoped belonged to the Levies. A group of people stood near the car. I thought they were Levies. The pilot asked me, 'What do you make of it? Is it OK to land do you think?'

'It looks all right to me,' I said. 'I think we can go in but I should keep the engines running after we get down. I hope that is one of the Levy vehicles by the strip.' With that he banked steeply, turned and came down on to the strip. We taxied up to the solitary vehicle with the engines popping in typical Dakota fashion. He braked gently, for fear of sticking in the soft ground, and pulled up near the Land Rover.

I was relieved to see the tall and bulky figure of Major Norman Smith, the second-in-command of the Levies, who came over to us, and, as I jumped down, shouted a hearty, 'Good morning.' In the open vehicle an Arab was sitting with what seemed to me a rather fixed look on his face.

'That's the Emir Bin Nami. I have just shot him,' said Norman.

'Oh really. Why?'

'Resisting arrest, silly coot,' he replied.

I walked over to Bin Nami who was the Emir in charge of the Saudi contingent and who looked distinctly uncomfortable; but he maintained a dignified pose, and we exchanged greetings. 'It's all right,' said Norman, 'it's only a flesh wound in his leg. We've patched him up. He was struggling to keep hold of that,' and he tapped a big steel chest which was in the back of the Land Rover.

I had a little further talk with the Emir Bin Nami, but the atmosphere was distinctly cool, and in the distance I could hear the crackle of small arms fire from the direction of Hamasah. As we stood there by the Land Rover the remaining Saudis came in other TOL trucks. There were fifteen of them, all dressed in the customary long white robes or shirts, and most of them had black cloaks decorated with gold braid. They all looked rather gloomy, but in the circumstances that was only to be expected. Norman and I helped Bin Nami into the aircraft and settled him down as comfortably as possible. The other Saudis got in as well. It was not until we were waving the aircraft goodbye that I realized that, in my excitement at this curious encounter, I had left my suitcase in the aircraft, and that for some time to come I would have with me only the clothes I stood up in. Norman suggested we looked at the Saudi camp.

I jumped into the Land Rover with him, and we went the half-mile or so across the plain to the group of tents in which the Saudis had been living. We walked around them, but there was not much to be seen, and the only thing of interest to us was the metal chest which was in the back of Norman's Land Rover. We forced the lock and found in it stacks of currency notes, which when we later counted them proved to amount to over one hundred and seventy-five thousand rupees. With the money were piles of paper and exercise books.

'That's all yours,' said Norman.

'All very well,' said I, 'but where can I put it? Can you give me a car?'

'Sorry, none to spare.'

I went walking on through the camp, and round the corner of the tented area I came across a wooden shelter in which I saw a blue Chevrolet saloon car. I got in, found the key was in the ignition switch, and it started. I backed it out and drove it over to Norman's Land Rover.

'Give me a hand with that chest,' I said, and we put it in the boot of the Chevrolet and locked it up.

'Now tell me what's going on.'

'We came in before first light. Tony Steggles got into Hamasah outskirts with his squadron without any difficulty, but he came under fire almost at once from the big new square house we call Bait Ageel. He has tried to negotiate but the other side keep shooting. They started it. While this was going on I came over here with the other squadron and rounded up the Saudis. They were just getting up for morning prayer. They could see at once that we were a hundred odd to only fifteen of them, and there was consequently no resistance until I went into that large tent and found Bin Nami struggling to get away with that great chest. God knows where he thought he could hide it. Anyway I went for him, he dropped the chest and got hold of me, pinning my arms. I had my hand on my pistol and I shouted, "Let me go or I'll shoot you." He didn't let go so I shot him through the leg. That fixed it. We bandaged him up and that was that. Now I must get back to headquarters. The Colonel is over at al-Jimi village.'

So saying Norman smiled and walked away followed by his men. They climbed into their Land Rovers and trucks and went off in the direction of al-Jimi. I got back into the Chevrolet and finding that its tank was half full of petrol followed in the tracks of Norman's squadron. As I came close to al-Jimi I could hear intermittent small-arms fire from the direction of Hamasah, and a cloud of white smoke was hanging by the houses of the village. The small group of vehicles which were those of the tactical headquarters of the Levies were tucked away behind a sand dune, about four hundred yards from the scene of the fighting. Standing on the dune, and looking at the village through his binoculars, was their Commander, Lieutenant Colonel Eric Johnson.

I got out of the car and went up to him, and we exchanged good mornings while he went on looking intently at the scene. In front of us there were two or three hundred yards of open, almost flat sand, at the other side of which there were a few very low, lumpy dunes and behind them the walls of the first mud houses of Hamasah village. Slightly to the left of these was the new square house which was called Bait Ageel. In this the Saudi Emir, Turki bin Ataishan, had lived for much of the time between 1952 and 1954. A little further to its right was another house which the Saudis had also occupied up to 1954, when they had moved out of the village in accordance with the Arbitration Agreement to the tented camp. Again to the right and behind this house were the buildings of the village itself and in the midst of them the squat mud tower of Shaikh Rashid bin Hamad's fort.

Eric Johnson was well known for his silent manner and at first said nothing, but before long he began to explain what was happening. He told me that the Levies had arrived before sunrise, one squadron going at once to the tented camp and the other entering Hamasah, where they were fired on. Captain Tony Steggles with another British officer had got into the smaller of the two houses which the Saudis had previously occupied, without opposition, surprising a few bedouin who had immediately run away. But almost at once they had come under fire from Bait Ageel. Soon after this they came under more intense fire from the village itself and also from the bedouin who had taken cover behind the wall of the neighbouring date garden.

Tony Steggles got all his men into defensive positions behind reasonable cover in and around this one house, and a small one next to it, but he had had to leave his transport in the open where it had already been damaged by small-arms fire. Both sides were therefore in good defensive positions and, we discovered afterwards, at one point the two sides were only twenty feet apart.

Eric told me an attempt had already been made to reach this squadron but they had been driven back by heavy crossfire from positions on the other side of the open ground. It seemed that this squadron was cut off from any support in daylight. The squadron which had come back with Norman Smith after the surrender of the Saudis had been put into position on the edge of al-Jimi village but for the time being they were unable to play a positive role. They were not able even to give effective covering fire, as the enemy were under good cover.

Eric told me that the village of Buraimi itself was reported to be quiet, and as usual its shaikh, Saqr bin Sultan al-Naimi, was trying to keep out of any trouble. He had never really committed himself whole-heartedly to the Saudis, but he had for some time ceased to take orders from the Sultan. His position with the Naim and Al Bu Shams tribes was no longer effective; and he sat almost besieged in the fort of Buraimi with only two or three of his followers and his pile of silver. His influence in the desert areas and particularly in Dhank some forty miles to the south, where he owned the main fort and much of the gardens, had, it was thought, largely evaporated. In normal times a tribe would get rid of a shaikh who had lost effective control. Saqr had so far managed to survive but this could not have lasted had not the Saudi presence and the Arbitration Agreement temporarily frozen tribal politics.

Eric's information was that his troops were up against a hard-core of some two hundred local bedouin, under the leadership of Shaikh Rashid of the Al Bu Shams and Shaikh Obaid bin Juma of the Bani Kaab. The tribesmen themselves were all Kaabis and Shamsis, all therefore subjects of the Sultan of Muscat. Eric said that shortly he would make another attempt to get a party across to the squadron in Hamasah, under cover of a smokescreen, to take in ammunition and evacuate a badly wounded soldier. It would be a hazardous operation because the extent of open country which had to be crossed was too wide to cover effectively with two-inch-morter-bomb smoke, which was all he had; and his own fire power was not adequate to keep the heads of the opponents down all the time. He did not have much hope that they would get through.

A Lincoln bomber had been flying over our heads for the past ten minutes, and I asked Eric what it was doing. He said he had a call on it for support from its machine guns, but in the present circumstances he could not use it, as the fighting was going on in the village, and it was vital to avoid any risk to non-combatants. Air power could have finished this skirmish in minutes, but Eric would not even consider it, rightly, for fear of the casualties to civilians. He was naturally unwilling to commit himself any further as to what he could do militarily; but without using the air support the military situation at least in daytime did not look so very hopeful to my lay eye. He said that just before they had set off on this operation, he had been told that I would be joining them, and that I would be responsible for any action necessary on the political side; and he asked me what I intended to do.

I said that it was too early to give him much idea. It happened that the principal 'enemy' leaders were very well known to me personally, and I hoped to make what use I could of this, and to get them talking before long. It might be possible at least to arrange a truce, if not a surrender. Eric said he was not interested in a truce, but if the enemy could be encouraged to surrender that would be fine, as far as he was concerned. He was anxious to avoid heavy fighting within the village, but he would have to do whatever was necessary to support and maintain contact with the squadron which was in the houses. He was in touch by radio with Steggles who reported so far one man dead and one severely wounded. Steggles also reported that he could hold his position without any difficulty; but unless he could be further supported, movement was impossible.

I said that I would do all I could to get in touch with the shaikhs. I told him that I intended to establish myself by a prominent tree just to the north of al-Ain village. Unless he heard to the contrary he could contact me there; and I would in turn keep in touch with him as soon as I had something to report. I explained that it was vital I should put myself well away from the Levies, as I hoped that the shaikhs in Hamasah and Buraimi would come over to see me and talk, provided I had no troops near me. I got back into my Chevrolet and drove off in search of the Abu Dhabi shaikhs. It was important to see them to explain my position.

I did not have far to go. Half-way across to al-Muwaiqi fort, the headquarters of Shaikh Zayed bin Sultan, the Ruler of Abu Dhabi's brother, I met Duda al-Amiri, a colourful character, riding his horse over the small dunes with his usual panache. I stopped the car, jumped out and waved. He waved back with his rifle, and galloped up to me shouting: 'Oh Bin Hender, what are you doing driving Bin Nami's car?' I explained that I was looking for Shaikh Zayed and his brother Hizza; and, bearing in mind his comment, I asked Duda to warn his villagers that if they saw the car it would be Bin Hender and not Bin Nami driving in it. He laughed and asked me to follow him, galloping off back towards the Levy headquarters as he spoke.

We had almost got back to where I had left the Colonel when he jumped off his horse and led it up a steep dune. I stopped the car and followed him on foot. We soon came to a point among the trees where we had a good view of the fighting; and there I saw Shaikh Zayed and his brother, looking at the scene through their binoculars, with a group of their men standing nearby.

I was greeted with a broad smile.

'What's going on?' said Hizza. 'Can't your troops get those Kaabis and Shamsis out of it?'

I explained the small numbers of the Levy force; and our unwillingness to use air support right in the village. Zayed laughed.

'Why don't you do what you did at Ibri? Go and talk to them!'

'I should love to but I can't get near them. Can't you help me?'

By this time we had walked down the dune, and Shaikhs Zayed and Hizza sat under a tree, and coffee was immediately produced by one of their followers.

'This is the Sultan's business and nothing to do with me,' said Shaikh Zayed. 'Hasn't he sent up a representative and where are his troops?'

'I am expecting the Sultan to send someone up, and some troops, not many, are on their way I believe. But I am not in touch with them, and all I can hope to do is to send across to the shaikhs over there, and try to get them to come over to talk. Couldn't you help me to do this?'

Shaikh Zayed turned to his brother, and had a long talk, at the end of which Shaikh Hizza turned to me.

'This is not our affair, as you know. Our people and our villagers are not directly involved; but I will come with you to al-Ain and see that you are all right, but we cannot take any part. It is not our business.'

I could not have hoped for anything more than this, and I thanked him, and suggested that we should go over to al-Ain straight away, to the place where I had promised the Colonel I would be. Shaikh Hizza agreed at once.

We drove across to al-Ain and stopped under the tree, just by the tall new fort. A rug was brought out from one of the houses for us to sit on, and Hizza's followers produced for us tea or coffee by turns.

The noise of small-arms fire continued throughout the morning from the direction of Hamasah; the Lincoln bomber circled endlessly over our heads; every now and then one of the villagers would come out and say something to Hizza. At one time we saw clouds of smoke in the direction of Hamasah, and then the noise of firearms increased for five minutes or so. Shaikh Hizza turned to me as we sipped the coffee, and said, 'As you are the Political Officer of the British Government here, we will do everything to help you on our territory, but we must not do anything in regard to the difficulty between the Omani government and their people. We do not have any position ourselves as regards this matter. But we are anxious to see a peaceful settlement. Although there is officially a boundary between our villages and the Sultanate side of the oasis, we are very close to our friends in Buraimi and Hamasah. We hope the fighting will stop, I have sent for two of our people, Muhammad bin Shaiban and Sultan bin Jazi, and they will stay with you as long as you are on our territory. I know you have arrived without your things, and they will provide bedding, food and anything else we can give you. I will stay not far away. Let me know if you want anything.'

I said how very grateful I was and asked him to thank Shaikh Zayed. Soon after he had gone Muhammad and Sultan, whom I already knew well and liked very much, came and after coffee asked what they could do. I said I needed very urgently to speak to someone from the Al Bu Shams or Naim. I knew that they were always coming over to the al-Ain market, and hoped they would be able to find someone. Meanwhile I wrote a note in my clumsy Arabic to Shaikh Rashid in Hamasah, asking him to come over to talk with me. A few minutes later Sultan came back and with him was a young Shamsi who was willing to act as a go-between. He was a relative of Rashid's. I therefore elaborated a bit on my note and asked him to explain that Rashid would be quite safe if he came to see me. I was willing to go part of the way across, if he wanted, towards Buraimi where he would be out of the direct line of fire. But we must talk, and if possible I wanted to talk to Shaikh Saqr. We must stop the shooting.

The Shamsi messenger was quite happy with this, but wanted me to drive him over nearer to Buraimi to save the walk; he would come back on a donkey or possibly in Saqr's car. We went over in the car to a point very close to Buraimi village. We could still hear the shooting over to our left but all seemed quiet in Buraimi itself and there were unusually few people about. There I dropped the Shamsi. I tried to give him some money but he was unwilling to take it. He said he was only too happy to come and go as often as necessary, he too wanted to stop the fighting.

I drove back to my tree and had coffee and fruit with my two friends, who looked after me wonderfully. They had spread rugs in the shade and from then on I was very comfortable. This was just as well because we had some long waits ahead of us as the messenger came and went. The distance was only about two miles, but Shaikh Rashid seemed to hold him inordinately at his end. The first sticking point was some sort of guarantee for the shaikh's safety if he came over. This was provided by Shaikh Hizza who said he would be answerable for Rashid's safe return if he came over.

As the day went on I became dragged into a negotiation through the Shamsi messenger, which was what I had wanted to avoid. It became clear that Rashid would settle for nothing less than a safe passage for him and a number of his people to Dammam in Saudi Arabia. Shaikh Saqr was apparently not reacting but it was made clear to me that his people were not involved in the fighting. I thought this might well have been true, as Saqr had tried to keep himself uncommitted. As I expected, there was no possibility of their agreeing to going to surrender to the Sultan in Muscat.

During one of the waits I drove over to see Eric Johnson at his headquarters. He said they had made a smokescreen and under its cover evacuated a badly wounded man, but they were not in a strong enough position to relieve the squadron which was in the village of Hamasah until after dark when he would have to put in a night attack if I had not succeeded in negotiating a surrender. However, he assured me he would not put in a night attack without first getting in touch with me. I pointed out that the early hours of darkness might be the best time to get the shaikhs to come over as movement would then be easier.

I realized I must patch up some kind of agreement before the night attack had to go in, as there might be considerable loss of life. I asked Eric to give me as much time as he could.

Eric said that a troop of Muscat infantry had come up to join him but there were very few of them and he did not think they would make any difference. I drove back thinking that I must fix something soon. I did not believe for a moment that Rashid would agree to go to Muscat, and even to mention it at this stage would put paid to his coming over. I resolved to say that this was what the Sultan had asked for when eventually we were face to face, but I knew that he would laugh the idea to scorn, and so would Saqr if ever I saw him. Towards sunset a relative of Rashid's came over and, while it was still not clear whether Saqr was willing to come, it seemed that Rashid would. Without giving away any plans I warned the cousin that things might get worse after dark, and it would be wise for them to come over as soon as possible. The sun set and no one came.

At about nine o'clock Norman Smith came over to see how I was getting on. He assured me that the night attack would not go in until he went back, and only then if it seemed unlikely that the shaikhs were coming at all, but it was planned for eleven o'clock and he must be back at HQ before then. He asked to be woken in time. He went a short way off, lay down and went to sleep. I had a long wait until eleven o'clock, and when it seemed that nothing was happening, I decided to give it another five minutes before waking him, then another five and so on until a wonderful sight, the very dim side lights of Saqr's old Ford car, came over the small dunes to our north-east (away from the battle area).

The car came straight over to us as we sat with hurricane lamps around us to direct it. Very slowly out clambered Shaikh Saqr followed by Rashid and the others. We shook hands and we all sat down and coffee came. I asked the shaikhs if they did not want to make peace with the Sultan, their Ruler. At this they exploded and Saqr made as if to go. I calmed him down, 'I have promised you your safety; you will not be sent anywhere against your will.' 'Then we will go to Dammam,' he said with dignity.

I discussed with them the details of a cease-fire. I said 'We must go at once to the Commander of the TOL and confirm the agreement with him to stop the fighting. When that is done we will discuss how many of your people want to go with you, and we will make suitable arrangements.' Rashid said that his men would not resist now, but it would be better for us not to move troops about until daylight.

Norman had woken up as soon as the car had comed to us, and after listening to this conversation said he would go over and tell the Colonel that I would be coming over with the shaikhs very shortly. I was anxious to get over to Eric and, taking the two shaikhs with me, drove behind Norman over the dunes. We were challenged by the sentries and Eric came over to us as we were getting out of the cars. 'Let me introduce you to the "enemy",' I said as we all shook hands.

We all sat down in the sand and a soldier came over with an Arab coffee pot and cup. I explained to Eric what had been agreed. He said he had a Dakota coming in first light. He would signal his headquarters in Sharjah and ask them to inform the Residency in Bahrain and the

Agency in Dubai so that arrangement could be made to send the party on to Saudi Arabia.

Eric had a tent put up for the shaikhs, and I went over to al-Muwaiqi to tell Shaikh Zayed and his brother what had happened. They were, of course, very glad. When I said that the shaikhs had refused to go to Muscat, Hizza commented, 'I do not know how you had the courage even to mention it.' This comforted me as I thought I had exceeded my authority in agreeing to their departure for Saudi Arabia, but I felt confident that the Political Resident would support my action, and in any case it was obvious that nothing would have persuaded them to go to Muscat. I now see in the official records that I was empowered to offer a safe journey to Dammam, but this is not my recollection, and I was given nothing in writing to this effect.

I left Shaikh Zayed and went back to al-Ain where a bed was waiting for me. By this time it was nearly three in the morning and we had been on the go for twenty-four hours. I was worn out, but before I went to sleep I arranged for a guard to be put on Bin Nami's car, having in mind the safety of the steel box locked in its boot.

The buzz of early morning flies woke me at six o'clock; and I drove over to the Levy headquarters. The Levies had spent the night in the open, since their tents had not yet arrived from Sharjah. By the time I reached them the shaikhs and their main group of followers had already been taken to the airstrip to await the Dakota which was to carry them to Bahrain. I suggested to Eric that he should send an officer to warn the headman, if such a person there now was, of Hamasah that he would be coming in with a party of troops to make a formal entry at about eight o'clock. Then I borrowed a razor and washed and shaved in the *falaj* stream. Eric invited me to join him for breakfast, and by the time this was over, his officers were getting the troops ready to drive across to Hamasah.

We discussed the curious question as to quite what we ought to do in the villages which after all were nothing really to do with us. We decided on a fairly formal entry into Hamasah with the small Muscat force, and a whole squadron of Levies, after which the Colonel should talk to the leading people. He would reassure them and say that all fighting had stopped and that officials from the Muscat government would be coming to Buraimi very soon. Then we thought we should inspect the forts of both Hamasah and Buraimi. I was particularly anxious to make adequate arrangements to secure Saqr's reputed treasure, which of course was the property of the Muscat government; and I wanted to enquire at once into a horror story that Saqr had kept a prisoner at the bottom of a deep hole in the ground for many months in the castle called 'The Castle of the Moat'.

Eric drove off at the head of the column while I came behind in one of his vehicles. After we had looked round the village and spoken to some of the people, the column moved on to Buraimi where Eric sent off an officer and some men to find and set free the miserable prisoner, while we went straight to the small fort in which Saqr had lived. We found this deserted except for the shaikh's bailiff, Sayyid Kamil, who was well-known to me. We asked him where the famous treasure was stored; and he pointed to a long low building across the courtyard. The double doors were locked but they gave way to the combined weight of Norman Smith and one of his soldiers. We filed in to find a long room lined with large wooden, brass-bound, Kuwaiti chests. Ten of these stood round the wall.

From earlier visits I knew where the shaikh's private apartments must be, and hoped we might find the key to the boxes there. The bailiff had the key to the main entrance of the private apartments and to the inner keep. Here on the first floor was the small concrete room in which the shaikh used to live alone. As he was always in fear of his life, at night he would lock himself in there against all comers. As his predecessor had been murdered he was always thought to be in fear himself of a similar fate.

We searched the room but could not find any keys. I asked the bailiff to send at once for a locksmith. While this was going on we heard that the prisoner had been found and the soldiers had pulled him out of the hole in which he had been incarcerated for eight months, without ever coming up. The hole was some forty feet deep and the floor at the bottom measured some ten by four feet. The poor man was in a fairly bad way physically, but was very brave. We saw he was well looked after, and a little later I went to see him. He made a good recovery.

The Colonel went on with his tour of inspection while Norman Smith and I examined the treasure. When we had the boxes open we found them filled almost to over-flowing with silver rupee coins dating well back into the last century; the coins and the notes amounted to one hundred and seventy-five thousand rupees. It was the thousand and one nights over again.

As an immediate precaution we had the bolt of the door mended, secured it with two large army padlocks and put a strong guard on the building. Eric and I kept the key of one lock each to demonstrate that neither of us separately had access to the treasure while we awaited the arrival of the Muscat government official. As yet only a junior officer had arrived with a small troop of infantry, and it was they who had been with us when we entered the village. A *wali* (governor) had been promised.

All the bedouin who had been engaged in the fighting against the Levies appeared to have left, but the majority of the villagers in both places were still there. In Buraimi the villagers clustered around us in a very friendly way. They took pains to point out that the treasure in Saqr's fort represented the taxes which the shaikh had taken from the poor villagers of Buraimi and Dhank over the years. It was really their money, they said.

We spent some time talking to the villagers and then went over to the Levy camp which had now been set up in the Abu Dhabi sector. There we were joined by Brigadier Baird, the senior British officer in the Gulf, who had come over by air from Bahrain to see what was going on. I showed him the box which had been the cause of the trouble between Norman Smith and Bin Nami. I was quite glad to hand over responsibility for this chestful of money and also the documents which were all returned to the Saudis.

The same plane had brought my suitcase and, later in the day, Sabir bin Muhammad drove in from Dubai with my Company Land Rover and a camp bed so that once again I felt equipped and mobile. Bin Nami's car I handed over to the Colonel. I had a long talk with Robert Baird and discussed the need to do something for the inhabitants who for various reasons were in rather a poor way. Robert promised to support any proposal which I might make towards helping them. In due course HMG provided enough money to clean the *falaj* system of the oasis, the underground water channels. I supervised this work over a period of six months. As a result the water flow increased dramatically.

That evening Shaikh Zayed asked us over to dinner in al-Muwaiqi; and after the meal we had a long talk over the events of the past days.

Shaikh Zayed had had a difficult two years. The Saudis over in Hamasah (they never occupied Buraimi itself) had plenty of money, with which they made themselves as popular as they could. Abu Dhabi was in the lowest trough of a long economic depression. There was no longer any real source of revenue, so that no public work could be carried out. Yet in this critical period the people retained their solid loyalty to their shaikhs.

I stayed on in al-Ain as Political Officer for HMG for another six months, on a temporary secondment from the Company, living in the top storey of a tower which later became a police post. In those days it stood alone in the desert away from any habitation, today it still stands in the middle of down-town al-Ain.

Shortly after the takeover of Buraimi a governor arrived from Ibri to be in charge of the Sultanate sector. His first sight of Saqr's silver seemed to astonish him; and he asked for my help in counting it.

I asked for a tailor from the village and set him making canvas bags each big enough to hold a thousand rupees. We borrowed a set of heavy scales from the market and by counting out one thousand coins and sewing them up we were able to use the bag as a measure to weigh against the rest. Nevertheless it took the best part of the morning before we had the whole treasure counted and securely sewn up. Eric and I then handed over both keys to the Governor in front of several witnesses; but he took them over, I thought, with some reluctance.

The new Governor of Buraimi was the son of the Governor of Ibri, and I had already met him. He seemed a capable young man. We soon struck up a friendly relationship, and I explained that, although I had no responsibilities on his side of the border, I was only too ready to help him in any way I could. With him had come a detachment of troops under command of my old friend Mike O'Kelly and I said to the Governor that we thought that the position in Buraimi and Hamasah itself would be secure, but we could not be certain of some of the areas to the south.

I had already collected some information about the political developments in the area. The bedouin and settled tribes who had been involved in the fighting had either gone back into the desert or, in the case of the Bani Kaab, to their villages in the mountain valleys, and the latter having now lost their leader, Shaikh Obaid, who had chosen to go to Dammam, were already grouping round another shaikh who was loyal to the Sultan. The Al Bu Shams had likewise lost their paramount, Shaikh Rashid, and were said to be grouping mainly behind Bin Rahmah who had a long history of loyalty to the Sultan (and incidentally a close relationship with Shaikh Zayed). The villages of Hamasah and Buraimi now came directly under the Muscat *wali*, and from now on had no recognized shaikh.

Away down to the south all seemed to be well in Ibri; but in the foothills between us lay the town of Dhank which had a mixed community, some of which had owed allegiance to Shaikh Saqr who had maintained a representative there and some to smaller shaikhs of little tribes or tribal splinter groups. I felt, as I had done in 1954 when we entered Ibri first, that until Dhank declared for the Sultan there would still be a dangerous situation in the Dhahirah district.

I suggested to the Governor that he and his father in Ibri should make enquiries about the loyalty of the people in Dhank, and do something to ensure that they declared publicly their allegiance to the Sultan. Later I had a visit from Colonel Cheeseman who had suceeded Percy Coriat as Commander of the MFF in Ibri. He agreed in principle to sending a squadron to Dhank as a demonstration of the Sultan's power, if he could be sure that this would be politically expedient.

The Governor of Buraimi made immediate enquiries about the position in Dhank, and in due course began to make contact directly with the leaders there, in particular with Salim bin Matar al-Azzizi, a former *wali* of Dhank under Shaikh Saqr but now showing loyalty to the Sultan.

On the days subsequent to the arrival of the Governor in Buraimi he and I again exchanged visits; and it soon became clear from the information we each were getting that the majority of the shaikhs of Dhank were only too anxious to show themselves to be loyal to the Sultan; but I was not surprised also to hear that they felt that it would be good to have this declaration of loyalty made at the same time as a visit of a strong squadron from the MFF. This seemed in keeping with local practice.

Colonel Cheeseman paid us another visit and it was agreed between him and the Governor that they would meet at a point where the main track from Buraimi to Ibri branched up the *wadi* towards Dhank, at nine o'clock on the following Thursday. Having now got the assurance of all the shaikhs that they could welcome a visit in force from the MFF, it was agreed that a squadron would then enter the town and would be entertained in the usual way by the leading shaikhs as their demonstration of loyalty to the Sultan. The Governor suggested that although I had no official position on his side of the border, it would be helpful if I would agree to accompany him.

Accordingly early in the morning on the appointed day I called at the Governor's fort and, together with Sabir and three of the Governor's personal staff, we set off in my Land Rover for the rendezvous. We reached it at about half-past eight and made ourselves coffee and had a breakfast of dates.

We waited there until nearly eleven o'clock in the shade of a thorn tree, but no troops came; and by this time I was becoming very anxious and thought that I should go to look for Cheeseman. The Governor said he would wait where he was since there was a considerable risk that I might miss the troops by taking a different track; there were a dozen different tracks between Ibri and Dhank. Someone must be there at the rendezvous in case the troops arrived without my seeing them.

Sabir and I set off alone over the bumpy gravel to Ibri, and we got there at about half-past one. I went straight over to the mess tent where I found the Colonel and several of his officers finishing lunch. I was tired and rather exasperated and I am afraid walked into the tent in a testy mood.

Cheeseman was surprised to see me and said that the plan had been cancelled by Muscat. He thought we would have been told. I explained the embarrassing and possibly dangerous position this created for the Governor of Buraimi. Cheeseman ordered his signals officer to raise Muscat on radio, and having failed to get through cheerfully agreed to come with me to Dhank, bringing a squadron of his men. I sent Sabir back to tell the Governor and soon we were on our way.

When his troops were ready Cheeseman asked me to join him in the leading vehicle, and we bumped our way in convoy in clouds of dust towards Dhank, necessarily rather more slowly than I had come down the same track in the morning.

It was nearly evening before we reached our rendezvous. The Governor was still where I had left him, but he had taken advantage of Sabir's return to send him into Dhank in my Land Rover to bring out some of the leading shaikhs. When we arrived they were sitting round him in a ring on the sand and seemed amiable and friendly enough.

He was overjoyed to see Cheeseman and the troops and the three of us drew aside to discuss the situation.

'It seems to be all right, except possibly for one small fort, and one quarter of the town, at the far end, but the shaikhs do not want anything to happen tonight. They would like us to come in tomorrow morning when all the forts will fly the Sultan's flag. I have given them one each. I am confident that it will go off smoothly,' said the Governor.

This was agreed and after a cup of coffee with the shaikhs we sent them back into the town in my Land Rover driven by Sabir. I remarked to Cheeseman and the Governor: 'Sabir seems to have captured the place on his own, do we really need to bother?' They laughed a little wryly.

We spent a quiet night by the tree; and on the following morning we set out in what I now had learned was the traditional order in this area. The Governor and one of his staff came with me in the front car, while the army was close behind. A number of the townsmen came out to watch and I drove straight up to the main fort, the Governor directing me, bumping over the rocks and gravel.

On this occasion there was really no cause for anxiety, but for some reason I was a bit nervous, and misjudging my speed I skidded to a halt in the gravel, the back wheels locked and we struck the main doors of the fort hard enough to break the door hinges on one side. The door collapsed inwards and I felt we had captured this castle. Fortunately this was taken as being rather amusing, and we all climbed out laughing. We were at once invited in to coffee and fruit, and warmly pressed to stay for lunch. Fortunately, also, there had been no one sitting behind that door.

While waiting for the meal we made a tour of the fort and the town. It had small but attractive gardens between the rocky cliffs, but there was something sinister and forbidding about such a rocky and overshadowed setting. After lunch we said goodbye to Cheeseman and thanked him for his spirited reaction; and the Governor and I went back to Buraimi.

While I was still in al-Ain and under the Political Resident's orders an important and welcome development took place. The Sultan of Muscat, accompanied by an army escort, made the long trek across the desert from Salalah in Dhufar to Fahud. He then entered Nizwa and from there made his progress to Ibri and finally reached Buraimi. He became the first Sultan to travel through the whole of the interior since Azzan bin Qais in 1859. Thus he ended the semi-autonomous position of the highland area centred on Nizwah and became the first Sultan of this century to rule the whole of Oman directly from Muscat. This important event is often played down or ignored altogether by writers on recent Omani history. The actual journey is described in colourful detail by that able writer James Morris, who accompanied the Sultan on his journey, and describes it in his book *Sultan in Oman*.

Shaikh Shakhbut entertained the Sultan and his officials with a splendid feast in the open (there was no building in al-Ain big enough for all the company which assembled). After this was over I was bidden to an audience with His Highness the Sultan, who graciously forgave me for persuading Colonel Coriat to disobey his express orders, and also for disobeying them myself. He then reverted to his usual friendly style. It was after all a long time since I had last seen him, and he said goodbye in a very charming way.

For two days the Sultan of Muscat stayed in camp near Buraimi and then he went by the new Wadi Jizzi track to his capital in Muscat and so completed a journey which changed the whole history of Oman.

In the summer of 1956 I returned to Bahrain. Thus I ended a long period of close association with development in the Trucial Coast and Oman, and one in which great advances were made, advances which were to alter the whole prospect for the future of the two countries.

Epilogue

The rest of my own story can be briefly told. In the spring of 1956 the Foreign Office and the oil company arranged to extend and formalize my secondment for three years, during which time I was in Bahrain but travelling a great deal round the Gulf. I made many trips to the Trucial Coast and some to Oman itself, especially to Ibri. I saw something of the way in which the Trucial Oman Scouts, as the Levies were now called, and the SAS helped to end the revolt which took place under the leadership of Talib and Ghalib in central Oman in June 1957. A small body of SAS gave the *coup de grâce* to the revolt by storming the rebel strongholds on the heights of Jabal Akhdar with the Scouts in support and the Omani forces. All this time Ibri remained loyal to the Sultan and our airstrip was used to bring supplies to the interior. Talib and Ghalib fled to Saudi Arabia in January 1959 and the Muscat government established its own governors and officials in the main centres of the interior. Oil was not to be found until 1964 and even then no real development by the government took place until 1970 when the present Sultan took over from his father, after deposing him in Salalah.

In February 1959 instead of returning to the oil company at the end of my three-year secondment, I was lucky enough to compete successfully in one of those rare over-age competitions for special entry as First Secretary into the Foreign Service. My new role took me back very happily to Abu Dhabi as Political Officer, representing HMG. Things were much the same with only the first stirrings of change evident. The arrival of a few cars and trucks did not make much difference, but a few houses had now been built (some with their own electricity generators) and the British Government had built a small office for the Political Officer, and a flat above it for him to live in. This made daily life easier and increased the possibilities of office work. I received no more letters

[175]

like the one I had once had from the oil company to ask why my (handwritten) accounts were so smudged, and to ask for clean copies. I had replied, 'The smudging is caused by sweat, please send a generator.' That had silenced them.

This pleasant stay in Abu Dhabi was cut short by illness which took me home. In October 1960, shortly after I left, oil was found in commercial quantities. For me there followed a posting to Jerusalem as Consul for Jerusalem and the West Bank; the latter was then not under Israeli occupation. It was an interesting but saddening experience. The tragedy of Palestine had further unfolded.

In 1964 I was posted to the Foreign Office for two years, partly to learn how the machine worked, an essential experience for a newcomer. After this I was in Bahrain from 1966-9 dealing Gulf-wide with our information effort. In 1969 I was appointed Her Majesty's Political Agent, the last in Qatar, and I was made Ambassador there in 1971 on the declaration of independence. I watched with admiration the strenuous work of Shaikh Khalifa bin Hamad, a very effective, hard-working leader, building up the country, active in every possible field.

In November 1974 I retired early from the Diplomatic Service at my own request as my short service had earned only a small pension and I felt that unless I found a new career soon I would be too old for anything. Shaikh Zayed generously invited me to live in Abu Dhabi and gave me a house there. After a short time spent on consultancy work, I was very glad to be invited by Shaikh Zayed to help with the collection of historical archive material for the Abu Dhabi government. The object was to obtain copies of material from all those countries which had political and trade links with the Gulf, starting with the Portuguese and Dutch. Naturally a large part of the more recent written material comes from London and New Delhi, especially in the nineteenth and twentieth centuries, and this is what concerns me. The work has taken me on visits to India and London where we arrange for material to be microfilmed and sent to Abu Dhabi where it is enlarged on to paper again, indexed and bound. This work takes place in the Old Palace in Abu Dhabi in which I first met Shaikh Shakhbut so many years ago.

In 1981 I had a year in London with the Council for the Advancement of Arab British Understanding (CAABU). One of my Arab friends said to me one day in his good but not flawless English, 'Edward, in CAABU you only preach to the convicted.' In fact we spread our net wider, but doing the job reminded me always of that penetrating remark.

After this I had a year and a half in the USA doing similar work. I thought the USA was fascinating, its people friendly and very hospitable, until it came to talking about Arabia. Then the majority listened politely but would not be persuaded to alter their views. The Zionist line is believed almost everywhere. There seems to me to be a gap, a fundamental misunderstanding between the West, especially the USA, and the Arabs. The West refuses even to recognize the existence of this gap and therefore sees no need to attempt to study it. It seems impossible to persuade the US Government that almost every act of theirs in the Middle East is based on this misunderstanding.

In Oman development was not remarkable until His Majesty Sultan Qaboos assumed the Rulership. Then it was very impressive particularly when one remembers that the country is extensive and largely mountainous, and further that the amount of oil found so far is very modest by Gulf standards. The way in which the country has been reunited for the first time for a century is of the greatest value to the progress of Oman as a modern state.

The later history of the Trucial States is common knowledge. Economic depression continued until oil was found there in 1960. Production followed and, at long last, the hoped-for income. In Abu Dhabi major development did not start until 1966 when, under the leadership of Shaikh Zayed, something approaching a miracle took place. The money coming in to Abu Dhabi was also used to help development in other separate Trucial States; until then only Dubai, by the exertions of its Ruler and merchants, had been able to expand at all before oil was found there.

From 1966 Shaikh Zayed as Emir directed the growth and development of Abu Dhabi, and within two years had to face the acute crisis caused by Britain's sudden decision to withdraw in 1971. The UAE did not then exist, and not only were its constituent parts divided, but they lacked nearly all the institutions of modern government. Most important of all was the almost total absence of educational establishments, which meant that there were very few people with the necessary training for government posts, and the people needed to teach and train nationals were wanting. Persuasion would not change the minds of the British, and Shaikh Zayed's statesmanlike decision to invite Shaikh Rashid and then the other rulers to join in making the UAE one state, involving for all of them the sacrifice of that most jealously treasured possession, sovereignty, saved the day; a new state was created. It advanced and grew at breathtaking speed, not without the difficulties which accompany all human endeavour. The exciting acquisition of new wealth created new expectations immediately, thereby pressuring those in charge to advance very quickly, often taking risks, experimenting much of the way, but always going forward. The fact that these great expectations have been so largely met in so short a time is a triumph.

When I look at the modern cities in the UAE and Oman I think of the pioneers, both nationals and expatriates. But for their work in those harsh days, living in tents in the desert with no electricity, working hard and under difficult conditions for years, none of this stupendous change could have happened. The UAE owes a great debt to these people. The leaders and the workforce together achieved marvels. Now that I am back once more, writing this in Abu Dhabi, I can say how exciting it is to see and live amidst all the new developments. In the days when I would visit Shaikh Zayed in his desert fort at al-Muwaiqi in the al-Ain oasis, I never dreamt that he would create this modern state. It is to him that the unity of these shaikhdoms is due. Such a success in joining separate communities into a whole has been a rare achievement.

Index

ARABIAN GULF

Dammam

BAHRAIN

Dhahran

QATAR

Doha

ₒDas

ₒ Dalma

Sir
O

SAUDI ARABIA

RUB' AL-KHALI
(EMPTY QUARTER)

TRACK OF PDO EXPEDITION OCTOBER 1954